Aboard the Fabre Line to Providence

· IMMIGRATION TO RHODE ISLAND ·

WILLIAM J. JENNINGS JR. & PATRICK T. CONLEY

Charleston · London
The History Press

Published by The History Press
Charleston, SC 29403
www.historypress.net

Copyright © 2013 by William Jennings Jr. and Patrick T. Conley
All rights reserved

Back cover, top: From Patrick T. Conley Collection.

First published 2013

Manufactured in the United States

ISBN 978.1.62619.229.4

Library of Congress CIP data applied for.

Notice: The information in this book is true and complete to the best of our knowledge. It is offered without guarantee on the part of the authors or The History Press. The authors and The History Press disclaim all liability in connection with the use of this book.

All rights reserved. No part of this book may be reproduced or transmitted in any form whatsoever without prior written permission from the publisher except in the case of brief quotations embodied in critical articles and reviews.

Dedicated to the mother of William Jennings Jr., Mrs. Margaret E. Jennings, who passed away on February 20, 2005.

CONTENTS

Preface 7
Acknowledgements 11

1. Making Providence Fine for the Fabre Line 13
2. The Early Years: 1911–1914 31
3. Disruptions of War: 1914–1918 47
4. Revival and Repression: 1919–1921 63
5. The Quota Years: 1921–1925 77
6. Steaming into History: 1926–1934 93
7. Passengers and Their Places of Settlement 117
8. Cargo of the Fabre Line 143

Fore and Aft: A Summation 151
Appendix 155
Notes 187
Bibliography 203
Index 213
About the Authors 223

PREFACE

I had originally hoped to write this preface at State Pier Number 1 on Providence Harbor, where the Fabre Line vessels docked for so many years. When I arrived there on September 13, 1974, however, I found that the gates had been locked and that my intention had been thwarted. I then moved southward down the harbor to an open spot on the waterfront where I could write. I had visited the old pier earlier that year and had thought, at the time, that it would afford an interesting and significant setting in which this preface could be written. On a pile of cement at the water's edge not far from the old state pier, I began to write.

To the north of where I sat, the old pier projected into the river. It presented a picture of desolation and inactivity. The shed on the wharf reflected a greenish and rusty color. Earlier that year, a fleet of tugboats had been using the south side of the edifice, the same side on which the Fabre Line's vessels used to dock, but now, even the tugboats had gone. The harbor itself displayed a panorama of stillness. From my spot of observation, I could not see a single vessel. Even across the bay at Wilkesbarre Pier, where so often tankers were moored, stillness dominated the scene. As I wrote, a slight breeze came from the northwest and cooled me. I took what I thought would be my final gaze at the old pier and the Providence waterfront and concluded that the days of the big ships at the port had long since passed.

As I gathered my materials together before leaving, I happened to glance once again southward down the harbor, and at this time, I observed a big white passenger vessel adjacent to the Municipal Wharf at Field's Point. My

Preface

thoughts ran back to the *Providence* and the *Patria*, two of the Fabre queens that so often graced the Providence waterfront. A single tugboat at the time was endeavoring to turn the big vessel about in the channel. As it slowly turned, I gazed, awestruck, at each of its passing sides. From its stern, I read the name *Victoria*, and I was reminded from recent advertisements in the media that it had been engaged by a local tour agency. As the tugboat slowly edged the passenger vessel to the quay, my imagination harkened back to the glory days of the Fabre Line.

Of the people who knew the Fabre Line firsthand and were interviewed in the early 1970s, when this research was first undertaken, many have passed on. So too have those who immigrated to America through the port of Providence on the Fabre ships; but many of their sons and daughters, and even more of their grandchildren and great-grandchildren, are still among us in southern New England, as well as in other sections of the country. Perhaps the publication of this study will add to their knowledge of their ancestors' journeys to this "promised land" of America. We hope that they and those who have an interest in Rhode Island's maritime past will enjoy reading this book.

WILLIAM J. JENNINGS JR.

Bill Jennings was a graduate student of mine writing his doctoral dissertation on legendary Pawtucket mayor Thomas P. McCoy when he began this study in the early 1970s. At that time, I was directing my newly established Rhode Island Ethnic Heritage Project at Providence College, a venture that led me to form eighteen Rhode Island Ethnic Heritage subcommittees after I assumed the chairmanship of the Rhode Island Bicentennial Commission in 1974. Since the Fabre Line was an immigrant passenger line, I naturally took an interest in Bill's research, offering constructive advice and engaging in an exchange of ideas. My Providence College colleague Matt Smith and I had already interviewed Thomas Farrelly, a former employee of the U.S. Customs Service at Providence, who processed Fabre Line immigrants. This interview was part of the Ethnic Heritage Project's attempt to gather oral histories as well as artifacts pertaining to the state's ethnic groups.

Preface

As Bill proceeded with his research, I assigned master's seminar papers on various aspects of twentieth-century Rhode Island immigration to some of my finest graduate students, and I shared these studies (cited in the bibliography) with Bill. In 1985, I began to edit the Rhode Island Ethnic Heritage Pamphlet Series, a tangible outgrowth of the Ethnic Heritage Program of 1976. Eventually, thirteen pamphlets were written by various authors that outlined the history of such Rhode Island ethnic groups as the Italians, French, Jews, Portuguese, Cape Verdeans, Greeks, Syrians, Lebanese, Armenians and Ukrainians—all of whom were represented in the passenger lists of the Fabre Line.

Despite this wealth of material, Bill's quasi-completed manuscript languished for years unpublished, a fate that also befell his insightful biography of McCoy. Then my wife, Gail, and I acquired the old Providence Gas Company/Imperial Warehouse building on Allens Avenue adjacent to State Pier Number 1, the berth of the Fabre Line steamships. It had been renovated in 1925 from a gas "purifier" plant to a storage facility by Samuel Priest in the vain expectation that the Fabre Line would increase its cargo-carrying capability.

In 2007, after expending nearly $7 million to again renovate the structure and secure its listing on the National Register of Historic Places, we opened a private cultural club on the building's fourth floor as an outreach program of the Rhode Island Publications Society. Because our building had been intended to serve as a warehouse for the Fabre Line and because the club attempted to attract and enroll a diverse array of members, Gail suggested that we call the new organization the "Fabre Line Club." Accordingly, we decorated our conference room with Fabre Line pictures, posters and other memorabilia, now depicted in this book, and our contractors, Al Beauparlant and Michael Dubois, even added many nautical touches, the most striking of which was a large replica of a Fabre Line steamship funnel mounted atop a huge stone fireplace.

From March 2007 through 2013, the Fabre Line Club staged sixty lectures on diverse topics and also held sixty book signings in this conference room to fulfill its cultural mission. Therefore, it is most appropriate that we use such memorabilia to illustrate this book, to which I have added considerable background based on my own histories of Providence and its people during the early twentieth century—the era of the Fabre Line.

Patrick T. Conley

ACKNOWLEDGEMENTS

We would like to express our gratitude to those who have aided in the completion of this study. We are indebted to Dr. John H. Kemble of the Frank C. Munson Institute at Mystic Seaport, Connecticut, and Pomona College in California for having directed research in the early phase of this study. Thomas L. Connelly of the U.S. Customs Service at Providence aided us in locating helpful materials and directed us to persons who remembered the Fabre Line. We are thankful to Thomas F. Farrelly and James F. O'Neil, former employees of the U.S. Customs Service, who knew the line firsthand and granted us interviews, in addition to Norton W. Nelson of Goff & Page, Inc., former agent of the Fabre Line, for his incisive recollections.

Finally, we would like to express our thanks to the staffs of the Providence Public Library, the Phillips Library and Archives at Providence College, the John D. Rockefeller Library at Brown University, the University of Rhode Island Library, the G. W. Blunt White Library at Mystic Seaport, the United States Custom House at Providence and the Diocese of Providence Archives.

Others who helped with the publication of this long-delayed project are Paul Campbell, archivist of the City of Providence; Dr. Hilliard Beller, editor for the Rhode Island Publications Society; photographer Frank Mullin; and Linda Gallen and Anna Loiselle, who not only typed the manuscript but also did extensive Internet searches for information. We are appreciative, also, for the sustained interest of The History Press in Rhode Island's history and heritage.

CHAPTER 1
MAKING PROVIDENCE FINE FOR THE FABRE LINE

The arrival of...[Fabre] ships...is a most interesting, inspiring, and instructive experience. Those who have never seen it have missed a sight well worth seeing.
— "When the Big Ships Come into This Port,"
Providence Magazine: The Board of Trade Journal

The city of Providence, Rhode Island, was invigorated at the beginning of the twentieth century with a new interest in maritime activity. Affairs relating to commerce and the sea had remained dormant at the port since its legendary "China trade" ended in 1841. Now, at the dawn of a new century, the city, state and federal governments undertook projects to improve the harbor at the head of Narragansett Bay and render the port more attractive for shipping. The city had railroad connections with the rest of the continent via the tracks of the New Haven Railroad, which, at this time, had nearly gained monopolistic control of transportation facilities in southern New England. The possibilities of a second major railroad connection by means of the Southern New England Railroad loomed large. This railroad was to tie in with the Canadian Grand Trunk, which entertained the idea of establishing Providence as its seaport terminus. In addition, the port had long-standing steamboat connections with New York via Long Island Sound. Providence was beginning to be referred to in the local press as "the Southern Gateway of New England."

At the same time, the port of New York was experiencing extreme congestion, so the federal government asked steamship companies to transfer tonnage and traffic to other ports. One of these companies—Compagnie

Aboard the Fabre Line to Providence

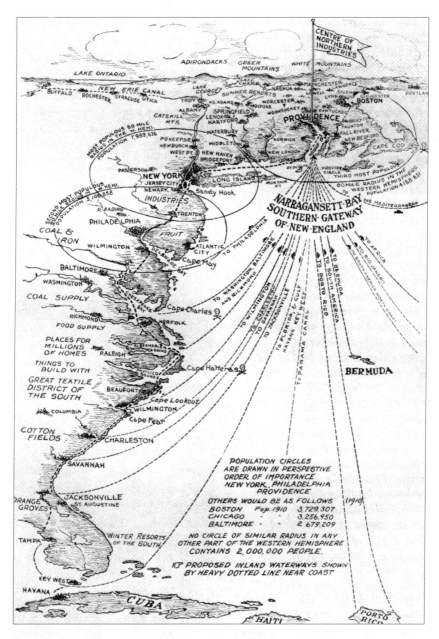

Typical of the optimism that infected the local business community with the arrival of the Fabre Line from France and the anticipated coming of Canada's Grand Trunk Railroad was this Providence-centered map, prepared by the Rhode Island Businessmen's Association. Extravagantly labeled the "Centre of Northern Industries," Providence was said to have a huge population and market for goods within an eighty-mile radius. In addition, all coastal and transatlantic routes led to Narragansett Bay, then styled as "the Southern Gateway of New England." What a difference a century makes. *Sketch from Manual of the Rhode Island Businessmen's Association, 1912.*

Française de Navigation à Vapeur, commonly known as the Fabre Line—responded to this request and, in 1911, chose Providence as the port where it would establish ancillary operations.

The city of Providence is situated at the head of Narragansett Bay. The harbor is the terminus of two important Rhode Island rivers, the Seekonk and the Providence. The former, which has its source near Worcester, Massachusetts, is known as the Blackstone River as far down as the falls in Pawtucket; the latter is formed by the merger of two smaller streams, the Moshassuck and Woonasquatucket Rivers. In the minds of those familiar with the waterfront during the second decade of the twentieth century, Providence Harbor was divided into two sections. The east side, the older section of the harbor, consisted of the entire waterfront between the east bank of the Providence River at Market Square to Fox Point as well as that which extended west along the bank of the Seekonk River to India Point, the latter named for its role in the Far East trade of the early nineteenth century. The west side began at the headwaters of the Providence River at Market Square and continued southward to Sassafras Point and finally to Field's Point. The Fabre Line initially used facilities on the east side of the harbor; it then used the state pier on the harbor's west side from the time the pier was opened in December 1913 until it was destroyed by fire in February 1931. The municipal pier at Field's Point, completed in 1916, accommodated the line during the final three years of its stay in Providence.

Providence's earliest important commercial project occurred in 1680, when Parson Tillinghast built the community's first wharf and warehouse. The town was a distant second to Newport during the colonial period, but Providence emerged as the state's leader after the American Revolution. Commerce was carried on from Providence with the Far East and West Indies during the years following independence until it faltered in the mid-1800s. For the remainder of the nineteenth century, coastwise commerce was the port's principal activity.[1]

Maritime interest began to revive at the port of Providence during the opening years of the twentieth century because the city and state had awakened to the possibilities that lay before them. In those years, the national government began work on a "harbor of refuge" and breachway at Point Judith. The harbor of refuge, or "breakwater," was completed to afford protection to the heavy commerce between ports in Narragansett Bay and New York via Long Island Sound. Some planners even envisioned connecting Narragansett Bay with both Massachusetts Bay and Long Island Sound by the construction of barge canals through Cape Cod. This scheme was part of a larger project advocated by the Atlantic Deep Waterways Association, which held its third annual convention at Providence in the fall of 1910. The association believed that the Atlantic Coast was not adequately served by the railroads, so it proposed a series of inland canals stretching from Maine to Florida. This ambitious endeavor was never fully realized locally except for the Cape Cod Canal, but its enthusiastic consideration by local leaders, as well as the city's willingness to host the convention, demonstrates the strong concern during these years for the redevelopment of commerce at Providence.[2]

At the same time, there were some in the community who were looking beyond merely improving connections between Providence and the two great commercial distribution centers nearby—Boston and New York. Local entrepreneurs proposed that Providence itself should be made a major distribution center of foreign commodities.[3]

In 1909, voters had authorized the issuing of a half million dollars in bonds to finance the acquisition and improvement of shore property within Providence Harbor, as well as in nearby Pawtucket and East Providence. The Greater Providence community was clearly on the move.

The actual preparation of Providence Harbor for transatlantic shipping began in earnest around 1910. From the very beginning, the project included all three levels of government—city, state and national. The city's share of the project consisted of the construction of a 3,000-foot-long quay or seawall (later to be enlarged to 4,750 feet) to serve as the municipal pier. The site chosen was Field's Point. The waterfront between Sassafras Point and Field's Point consisted of sandy flats jutting out at its southern extremity into the main shipping channel, land that was then of no use to commerce. However, it had been a major recreational area. Casualties of its commercial modernization included a public park called Field's Point Farm, a Revolutionary War breastwork known as Fort Independence and Colonel S.S. Atwell's Clam House, a regionally famous shore dinner hall whose oysters were plucked from the adjacent shallow waters.

The role of the state in this harbor project involved gaining acquisition of riparian rights along the waterfront in preparation for the construction of wharfs and piers. At the same time, almost the entire waterfront suitable for the type of development that might accommodate transatlantic shipping was, by lease or ownership, in the hands of private investors. The state began to acquire some of this waterfront property by purchase and eminent domain.[4]

The federal government's share of the project consisted of straightening the channel and dredging it to a width of six hundred feet and a depth of thirty feet at mean low tide from the lower anchorage in the inner harbor to deep water. By agreement, the federal government was not obliged to undertake its share of the project until the city and the state had made substantial headway.[5]

It was apparent to all at the outset of the second decade of the twentieth century that the Providence business community was very much interested in increasing maritime activity by securing oceanic commerce, and major steps were being taken to render the seaport more attractive to those who directed transatlantic steamship companies, such as the owners of France's Fabre Line.

The Fabre family had been involved in trade and shipping in the Mediterranean Sea since the fifteenth century and had accumulated great wealth. Cyprien Fabre (1838–1896), heir to this mercantile tradition, founded his own company, the Société Cyprien Fabre et Cie, in 1868 at the age of thirty. At first, he bought a few sailing ships to trade along the West African coast. Next, he turned his attention to innovative steam-powered vessels by purchasing the 1,400-ton *Commassie* in 1874 from the Dixon Company of Middleborough, England. By 1879, that ship had been renamed *Patria*, and Fabre had acquired other steamers: the 1,700-ton cargo vessel *Provincia*; the *Lutetia* and the *Gallia*, both 1,200-tons; and the 850-ton *Massila*. During that year, sailings were inaugurated on a weekly basis from Sete and Marseilles to Oran, Algeria, via Alicante and Valencia, Spain. Fabre also developed a variety of other Mediterranean sailing routes.

In March 1879, Fabre sent the *Patria* on an experimental voyage from Marsailles to Liverpool, and in the following June, he sent the *Provincia* on another trial voyage to Antwerp, Belgium. On December 26, 1879, the *Provincia* sailed again from Marseilles bound for New York, Fabre's first transatlantic venture. These experimental trips apparently proved to be unprofitable, so in early 1880, the *Provincia* was sold to the Compagnie Générale Transatlantique (known popularly as CGT and called "the French Line"). No further experimental sailings were attempted for another year, until Cyprian Fabre completed a reorganization of his maritime business.

The Compagnie Française de Navigation à Vapeur, also known as the French Steam Navigation Company or the Fabre Line, was founded in 1881 by Cyprian Fabre with a capitalization of 15 million francs. Fabre's contribution to the company's capital stock consisted of his previously acquired steamers: *Gallia*, *Lutetia*, *Patria* and *Syria*. Immediately after its business consolidation, the new company purchased four other steamers, including the 2,500-ton *Scotia*. This newly built vessel may have undertaken

Aboard the Fabre Line to Providence

Cyprien Fabre (1838–1896) founded the Fabre Line in 1881 at Marseilles, France, in keeping with his family's centuries-old mercantile tradition. The Fabres had been involved in trade and shipping in the Mediterranean Sea and the West and East Indies since the fifteenth century. It is fitting that the flag of the Fabre Line—white with a light blue cross—is identical to the municipal flag of Marseilles. *Portrait from Wikipedia.*

three experimental voyages between Marseilles and New York in 1881, although there is no clear evidence of these voyages. However, the *Scotia* and its sister ships, *Britannia* and *Asia*, were plying this route in 1882, along with ships of the French Line. In the autumn of that year, the latter company withdrew from the route, much to the satisfaction and advantage of the Fabre Line, whose New York run was in full swing by 1883, when the line made thirteen crossings, carrying 24 first-cabin and 4,569 steerage passengers westbound. Also in 1883, the line commissioned the 2,800-ton *Burgundia* for this route and soon began service to South America, with the *Scotia* again cast in the role of the pathfinder. This traffic would be discontinued in 1905, after the line had become firmly established at New York.

IMMIGRATION TO RHODE ISLAND

The New York service was increased in 1886 from fifteen to twenty voyages per year. This expanded activity between Marseilles and the American port necessitated the transfer of the *Scotia* from the South American service. Misfortune struck the line in March 1887, when the *Scotia* ran aground on Long Island. It was refloated a month later, taken to New York and sold.

Sailings between New York and Marseilles were again increased in 1891, with the annual number being raised to twenty-six. During that year, the three-thousand-ton *Massilia* was commissioned for the New York run. The Fabre Line added no further tonnage until 1902, although the *Rugia* was purchased from Germany's Hamburg-American Line in 1895 and the *Chateau Yquem* from the Campaignie Bordelaise in 1897. The latter was renamed *Gallia*, and the *Rugia* became the *Patria*. This ship should not be confused with the larger and more noteworthy *Patria*, built by Fabre in 1913, that became a frequent visitor to Providence.

In 1887, establishing what might be termed the French connection, the company instituted Marseilles–New Orleans service, a run that continued until 1903. Despite the death of its entrepreneurial founder at the age of fifty-eight on March 8, 1896, the Fabre Line continued to grow and prosper.

British, German and Italian steamship companies running between the Mediterranean and New York placed increasing numbers of ships in service during the opening years of the twentieth century. Keeping abreast of the times, the Fabre Line commissioned the 5,700-ton *Roma* in 1902, the 4,900-ton *Germania* in 1903, the 5,500-ton *Madonna* in 1905 and the 6,700-ton *Venezia* in 1907. All four steamers had accommodations for more than fifty first-class passengers, in addition to several hundred in steerage.[6]

The facilities for the accommodation of steamships at the port of New York had become extremely congested during the opening years of the twentieth century. Chaos had been allowed to reign unchecked along its waterfront in the years prior to 1900, and most of the wharfage and terminal facilities had come under the control of private enterprise. By 1910, the city had regained possession of most of its waterfront facilities, but their supervision was rendered negligible by the long-term leases that were granted for those properties. After 1910, New York adopted a more effective procedure: leases would be issued for a period of ten years only, with the privilege of renewal provided that the lessee made "permanent and extensive" improvements to the piers. The city could repossess the piers before the expiration date upon payment of an appropriate sum toward the cost of improvements made by the lessee. This new waterfront policy permitted realistic planning toward the reconstruction and improvement of harbor facilities, but unfortunately no major changes occurred at the port prior to World War I.[7]

The congestion at the port of New York was most pronounced with regard to terminals. Passenger and, especially, freight connections between the steamship lines and the railroads were extremely difficult as a consequence of the peculiar geographical setting of the island of Manhattan. Only the New York Central and the New Haven Railroads had access into the commercial heart of the city. Moving passengers and freight between the steamships and the railroads required the use of lighters as well as teams of horses to draw railroad cars to certain terminals, and this procedure added to the general cost of transportation via the port of New York.[8]

Congestion was not peculiar to the New York port; it was a problem experienced by many large seaports. However, the problem at New York at this time was acute. A marginal railroad along the waterfront, with spur tracks to the various piers, became a necessity. This congestion at our nation's major seaport gave rise to various railroad-owned Long Island Sound steamboat lines (most of them subsidiaries of the New Haven Railroad) that avoided this congestion by docking at the lower tip of the city. "Their terminals on Manhattan Island enabled them to function as 'practically lighterages lines' from the railheads at the Sound ports to the New York piers," writes railroad historian W.L. Taylor.[9]

Studies conducted by representatives of the city, state and federal governments recommended that steamship companies do their part to relieve the congestion at New York by sending their surplus tonnage to other ports. Far more important than the glut of products, however, was the massive migration of people. From the 1880s onward, the sources of American immigration changed from western and northern Europe to the southern and eastern sectors of that continent. This so-called new immigration reached unprecedented levels during the first decade of the twentieth century. In 1905, the number of foreign arrivals passed the million mark for the first time; it peaked in 1907 at 1,285,349, and it registered over 1 million six times prior to 1915, when the world war cut it drastically. New York's Ellis Island bore the brunt of this influx, an overload that Providence and other ports came forward to relieve.[10]

Although the Fabre Line's New York terminal was located in Brooklyn, the conditions of congestion and poor connections with the railroads existed there, as they did on Manhattan Island. The problem with respect to rail connections may even have been more acute in Brooklyn, inasmuch as the trunk lines channeled their tie-ins near Manhattan. This serious congestion at the port of New York was the major factor prompting the line to direct some of its business elsewhere.[11] The Fabre Line responded to this situation by considering its options. After a careful study of the advantages offered by seaports between Portland, Maine, and Charleston, South Carolina, the company selected Providence as the port offering the greatest potential for its passenger operations.

Basic reasons for the Fabre Line's choice of Providence were its awareness of the major improvements that had been made recently to the city's harbor, plus the general rebirth of enthusiasm for maritime commerce that was exhibited there by city, state and business leaders. These were the most important factors in the company's decision to transfer some of its activity to Providence. There were, however, other considerations.

By the beginning of the second decade of the twentieth century, the New Haven Railroad had gained nearly monopolistic control of transportation facilities at Providence, and there was little doubt that the Fabre Line could arrange a satisfactory agreement respecting through rates with the railroad. There was also an extremely good possibility that within a short time the port would have a second major rail connection that would tie into the Canadian Grand Trunk. It seemed certain to all in 1910 that this prospective newcomer, the Southern New England Railroad Company, would be in operation soon, with Providence as its seaport terminus. It was projected that the line would tie into the Northern New London Railroad and eventually, via the Central Vermont Railroad, connect with the Canadian Grand Trunk. Under the terms of the charter granted by the State of Rhode Island to the Southern New England, "the location of said railroad" was to be filed with the state before July 1, 1911, and the construction was to be completed before July 1, 1915. The incorporators of the new railroad included Charles M. Hays, director of the Grand Trunk, who was seeking, via the new road and the port of Providence, a relatively ice-free seaport terminal for his Canadian line.

Needless to say, the New Haven Railroad, which at this time was just completing its efforts to gain monopolistic control of rail transportation in southern New England (if not all New England), vehemently opposed the establishment of the second railroad. The argument advanced by the New Haven twenty years later, when again the possibility existed that the Southern New England Railroad would be established, is both interesting and applicable to the time period now being considered:

> *In the early days the service for Providence was provided by several independent railroads. As the railroads improved their service and increased their traffic the several independent companies came under a common control*

Aboard the Fabre Line to Providence

This cartoon, drawn by noted *Providence Journal* illustrator Milton R. Halladay, depicts New England in the grip of the monopolistic New Haven Railroad and its talented and tenacious president Charles S. Mellen. During the tenure of the Fabre Line at Providence, the New Haven's control over railroad and steamship transit continued, forcing Fabre to adjust to this reality. However, in 1914, the federal government reined in the runaway New Haven, at least forcing it to relinquish its control over Rhode Island's urban and suburban streetcar lines. *Cartoon from the* Providence Journal.

IMMIGRATION TO RHODE ISLAND

Charles Melville Hays, a wealthy and dynamic Canadian entrepreneur, posed the greatest challenge to the New Haven Railroad's transportation monopoly. His proposal to bring the Grand Trunk (later the Canadian Pacific) Railroad to Providence's ice-free harbor would have greatly impacted both the city and the Fabre Line by giving the French steamship company direct access to Quebec, thereby allowing both the city and the line to tap the trade of Canada. This plan received a fatal blow when Hays went down with the *Titanic* in April 1912, prompting some observers to call the Grand Trunk "the railroad that perished at sea." *Photo of Hays's portrait from Larry Lowenthal's* Titanic Railroad.

as a public necessity, so that the through routes that are now available would be possible and that the terminal facilities could be used for all the traffic without additional expense to the shipper...

...The advantages enjoyed by Providence through being served by a single railroad are now sought by the ports served by several railroads. Expensive belt line railroads are even operated through the public streets at some ports to connect the piers and industries with several railroads.

With a suitable harbor, reasonable port regulations and port charges, proper terminal facilities, and adequate rail service to the interior, all available, the next step in the development of the port is to induce the steamship lines and the import and export traffic to use the port.[12]

Unfortunately for the embryonic Southern New England Railroad, Charles M. Hays was lost on the *Titanic* (April 15, 1912), and the railroad lost its most aggressive champion. The work of surveying and acquiring a right of way and of building roadways and bridges continued for a time, but eventually, all activity came to a standstill. On June 30, 1926, after several extensions by the general assembly, the railroad's charter finally expired. The demise of the Southern New England has prompted historians of the project to describe it as "the railroad that perished at sea."[13]

Aboard the Fabre Line to Providence

This 1912 photo shows how close the Grand Trunk got to Providence Harbor via the Southern New England Railroad before the *Titanic* and the New Haven Railroad's Charles S. Mellen halted its progress. It depicts the construction of a tunnel under Broad Street parallel to the New Haven's Harbor Junction tracks, less than a mile from the river. Mellen was later indicted by a grand jury under federal antitrust statutes for his role in pressuring the Grand Trunk to halt its road construction into Providence. He was not convicted. *Photo courtesy of the* Providence Journal.

Another feature of the port of Providence as seen by the officials of the Fabre Line was the existence of large Italian and Portuguese communities in the vicinity. Thriving Italian communities had developed in the Federal Hill, Silver Lake and North End sections of Providence, while at the same time large numbers of Portuguese were settling in Providence's Fox Point, in the East Bay towns of Rhode Island (especially East Providence) and in nearby Fall River and New Bedford. Various importers catered to these immigrants—especially the Italians, who then had a firmer foothold in the area than did the Portuguese—by importing their native foodstuffs. These imports came through the port of New York, but it was reasonable for the Fabre Line to expect that these same goods could also be imported through Providence once the company had established operations there. This new terminus would lessen the congestion at the company's Brooklyn pier, and with the cost of transportation to Providence via train eliminated, selling prices would fall. These new conditions would then serve as a stimulus to expand the line's current volume of trade.[14]

Moreover, many of the passengers debarking at the Fabre Line's New York terminal made rail connections to southern New England, so a stop at

Providence would give the line a strong advantage over competition for this particular immigrant traffic, especially the Portuguese. Additionally, many of the immigrants feared disembarking at New York—a city of intimidating size where a language other than their own was spoken. These immigrants were easy victims for the more highly developed "wolves" of the metropolis who were eager to separate them from their money. At Providence, friends could meet them at the boat.[15]

It is uncertain whether the managers of the Fabre Line believed that their activities at the port of Providence could ever be sufficiently developed to enable the line to quit New York. No doubt this possibility was given serious consideration. It is much more probable, however, that the line was simply attempting to expand its current business and reduce its involvement in the stifling congestion at New York by calling at Providence. It would seem that the line discounted Boston and points north of Cape Cod because vessels continuing on to New York from these ports would have to deal with the dangerous shoals that extend far to the south of Nantucket. Steamers could call at Providence and then sail on to New York without such great difficulty. If the line was considering the eventual transfer of its operations to Providence, that transfer could be effected gradually and smoothly with some of the company's facilities already established there. Providence's rail connections with the major trunk lines at this time were as fine and efficient as those of New York.

It also appears that the Fabre Line had plans to establish direct sailings between Italy and Providence, using its smaller and older vessels. Direct service between Italy and New York was maintained by other lines at this time. Nonetheless, Marseilles remained the port of embarkation for ships calling at Providence throughout the Fabre years.[16]

On March 7, 1911, the U.S. Congress passed a bill authorizing the survey and examination of Providence's harbor and its environs for the purpose of dredging a thirty-foot channel. At the same time, the Fabre Line officially announced its intention to call at Providence. Rumors had been circulating throughout the city for months that the line was ready to come to the port as soon as it became definite that the channel would be dredged. The announcement of Fabre's decision was made by former Lieutenant Governor Frederick H. Jackson, who—along with Mariano Vervena, the Italian consular agent at Providence—had been instrumental in convincing the line of the port's merits.[17]

The *Providence Journal* reported that the *Madonna* would sail from Marseilles on June 3, 1911. The ship would visit Italy, call at the Azores and

Frank H. Jackson, a Providence businessman and Republican politician, was instrumental in bringing the Fabre Line to Providence. Jackson, a native of Oneida Town, New York, served as the state senator from Providence (at that time, each municipality had only one) and as lieutenant governor from 1905 to 1908. *Photo from the Providence Journal Almanac for 1903.*

Henry Fletcher, mayor of Providence from 1909 to 1913, lent strong official support to the effort to attract and maintain the Fabre Line at the port of Providence. Fletcher, a Republican, had close ties with the local business community. *Photo courtesy of the Providence City Archives.*

then continue on to Providence and New York. The vessel was expected to reach Providence on June 16, 1911, and dock at the New Haven Railroad's Lonsdale Wharf on the east side of the harbor in Fox Point. Dredging operations began there immediately to accommodate the *Madonna*.[18]

The announcement of the Fabre Line's impending arrival was enthusiastically received throughout the greater Providence area. Governmental and commercial leaders issued statements of support. Perhaps the most colorful response to the Fabre announcement was a facetious letter written to the editor of the *Providence Journal*:

> *The Fabre Line announces that its steamer "Madonna" will arrive at Providence on or about June 16th next…Why not make the arrival of the steamer an occasion for riotous joy and feasting?*
>
> *Here is something of real benefit to the city and State and anticipating the selection of committees, soliciting of funds and formation of programs, I rush in, angel-unlike, and urge and proclaim a plan.*
>
> *Before the Legislature adjourns, secure an appropriation of at least $25,000. To accomplish this, authorize a few more committee clerks if necessary. Then get the City Council to appropriate $15,000 more, and let the sweeping of the Moshassuck go over another winter so as to save money. Issue a few bushels of buttons showing the tricolor of France entwined about Neptune's trident with the motto "Macaroni for the Masses—Olive Oil for All." Plan to run "scare headlines" in all newspapers, such as "Marine Splendor Again Crowns the Glory of the Port," "Triumphant Procession of the French Leviathan Up the Bay," "Bedlam of Tooting Whistles Greets the Guest from the Mediterranean."*
>
> *Have the Board of Trade get out a bulletin showing the differentials between Providence and Paris via Marseilles and Providence and Paris via Cherbourg with resultant effects upon farm rents in Foster. Have Infantry Hall inspected by the Steamboat Inspectors and then hold meetings, the first day with such speakers as a Brown University professor on Analytical Geometry, [Gifford] Pinchot on Conservation, Dr. Cook on the North Pole, Champ Clark on Annexation of Canada, a Turkish missionary on the harem skirt, Hobson on our war with Japan—with the Governor, the Mayors of Rhode Island cities, Overseers of the Poor, the Collector of the Port, the Superintendent of Hacks, the Dog Officer and the Inspector of Milk sandwiched in between and Dr. [Lucius] Garvin to close with just a few words on the single tax. Let ex-Senator [Albert K.] Beverage of Indiana devote his second and third days to Child Labor.*

Aboard the Fabre Line to Providence

Arrange a mammoth torchlight parade to include veterans of the late War with Mexico (if there has been one), suffragettes, portable searchlights, students and ship-carpenters.

Construct a statue of Liberty on Fuller's Rocks, using as a model the figure of a female strap-hanger on the Eddy Street line.[19]

The initial enthusiasm was tarnished somewhat when the company announced that the line would not handle freight at Providence because of the insufficiency of wharf facilities. The steamers would disembark passengers, but all incoming and outgoing freight would have to be handled at New York.[20] Gloom did not persist for long, however, because two days later, on March 25, 1911, news came that the company had decided to advance its initial arrival from New York to May 13, 1911.[21]

The steamer *Madonna* entered Narragansett Bay on that May Saturday amid thick fog, "cheering crowds, booming cannon, and screeching whistles

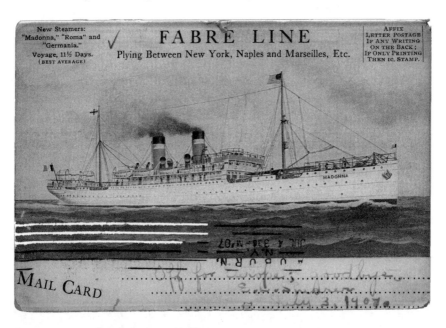

This 1907 postcard depicts the *Madonna*, built in England in 1905 for the Fabre Line. It sailed on its maiden voyage from Marseilles via Naples to New York in April 1905 and continued on that route until it became the first Fabre ship to carry passengers from Providence on May 13, 1911. The *Madonna* originally had accommodations for 54 first-class passengers and 1,650 third-class, or steerage, passengers, but in 1912, Fabre added facilities for 60 second-class travelers. The *Madonna*'s final visit to Providence came on March 31, 1925; thereafter, it was used on the West African Coast before entering an Italian scrapyard in May 1934. *Postcard from Patrick T. Conley Collection.*

and the dipping of the Stars and Stripes." It arrived in the harbor at 9:40 a.m. but could get no closer than thirty-five feet from the New Haven–owned pier at Fox Point that had been made available for the steamship company's temporary use. With the *Madonna*'s keel resting in the mud, a gangplank was laid alongside for the public and passengers to board the vessel. Tours were conducted during the remainder of the morning, and during the afternoon, a luncheon reception was held on board and attended by important members of the community. D.H.G. Jones of James W. Elwell & Company, New York agents for the Fabre Line, emphasized the line's desire for a channel depth of thirty-five feet from wharf to ocean—the first of many demands he would make of the Providence community during the next few years.

The *Madonna* pulled away from the dock at 6:45 p.m. and steamed down Narragansett Bay, ultimately bound for Marseilles, with forty-two first-class and four hundred steerage passengers, most of them destined for the Azores to take part in the Festival of Jesus Christ, which would be observed there on May 20. The ship was navigated in and out of Providence by the state's most famous pilot, Captain W. Talbot "Tal" Dodge of Block Island.[22]

A new era in Providence's maritime history had begun, finally fulfilling the dream of J.B.G. Fauvel Gaurand, a French vice-council residing in South Providence in the mid-nineteenth century, who tried, persistently but unsuccessfully, to establish a steamship line between France and Providence.[23]

CHAPTER 2

THE EARLY YEARS

1911–1914

During the early years of its operations at the port of Providence, the Fabre Line pressured local officials for improvements within the harbor itself and in its channel. Without question, the most serious deficiency was the lack of adequate wharfage facilities that would enable the line to handle cargo. The problem remained unsolved until December 1913, when the new State Pier in South Providence at the foot of Public Street was placed at the line's disposal. Modern facilities at the new pier resolved that issue. Eight months later, in August 1914, the European continent became embroiled in a war that would seriously affect the line's sailings until the termination of the conflict in November 1918.

In these early years, the Fabre Line and the New Haven Railroad were at odds over Fabre's use of the New Haven wharf, and the line threatened to quit the city if matters were not resolved to its satisfaction. Yet in spite of its arrogant attitude toward both the Providence community and the railroad, Fabre gained a firm foothold at the port during these early years of operation.

Ten days after the line inaugurated service at Providence in May 1911, dredging began in the harbor in an effort to prevent a repetition of the embarrassment caused when the *Madonna* struck bottom on its first arrival.[24] The success of this effort proved questionable. The *Madonna* did not scrape its keel in the mud on its second trip to the city on June 16, 1911, so the line's officials congratulated the community for its recent efforts when the ship docked. Those kudos were premature. On July 1, the *Germania*, another of the line's steamers, stirred up mud from the harbor bottom as it arrived. The ship had earlier struck the mud flats off Sabin Point, near Riverside, when coming up the bay, although the contact had not been serious enough to harm it or impede its progress.[25] On August 10, the *Madonna* struck bottom again while at its slip, and it had to await a turn of the tide before sailing.[26]

Despite the apparent inadequacy of the dredging, Fabre's complaints during these early years were more often directed toward the lack of facilities at the New Haven–owned wharf, which the line was using on the condition that it not load or unload cargo of any consequence, save small packages. Flare-ups occurred twice, embroiling officials of both companies as well as the local government. These disputes concerned the accommodations provided for landing immigrant passengers and the per capita charge that the railroad levied on the Fabre Line for passenger disembarkation.

The agents of the steamship company were apparently pleased with the initial work toward improving the port at Providence and announced that service there would become permanent. The line also announced that it would extend sailings to include calls at Almeria, on the southern tip of Spain, though these stops would be discontinued during the harsh winter months between October and February.[27]

The Fabre Line was plagued during its initial months at Providence with having its passengers examined for cholera. An epidemic had broken out in southern Europe, and an inspection for this disease meant delay for the line's steamers entering the United States from ports declared to have been infected. Marseilles, Lisbon and the whole of Italy were among the afflicted areas, and the government directed that all immigrants from these regions were to undergo a bacteriological examination and a five-day observation period before being allowed to disembark at United States ports. In Providence, these examinations were conducted under the general supervision of Dr. Charles V. Chapin, Providence's nationally renowned superintendent of health, with the tests being processed at Brown University.

It was first believed that all passengers would be detained for five days of observation aboard the incoming vessels, since there were no detention quarters at the port of Providence. It was later explained, however, that the rule requiring the five-day detention period had been made before the development of the bacteriological test for cholera. Since the medical profession considered the test to be effective immediately in identifying the presence of cholera, the period of observation, said Dr. Chapin, was unnecessary. The change in procedure was a favorable break for the company as well as for the port of Providence. The Fabre Line had intimated that if the

Immigration to Rhode Island

This faded postcard/poster is a very early indication of the connection between the Fabre Line and the James W. Elwell Company of New York. The Elwell firm, founded in New York City in 1821, served as general agents for the line during Fabre's entire time at Providence. The advertisement depicts the "new" Fabre steamship SS *Sant'Anna*, which was built in 1910 but never visited Providence. Commandeered as a troop transport during World War I, the vessel was sunk in 1918 off the coast of Tunisia with a loss of over five hundred lives. *Conley Collection.*

detention period was required, the company might be forced to temporarily withdraw from Providence and carry its passengers to New York, where there was an adequate quarantine station. This situation revealed the need for such a station in Providence, and by 1914, the city obtained the old navy cruiser *Newark* to serve that function. These precautions were for naught because the Fabre Line transported no cholera cases to Providence, and by the end of the summer, the crisis had passed.[28] It was the first time—but not the last—that the company experienced an inconvenience of this nature during its days at Providence.

During 1911, the Fabre Line made a total of ten inbound and seven outbound calls at Providence. The Fabre vessels that called at the port were the *Madonna*, the *Germania*, the *Venezia* and the *Roma*. These were the largest ships that had ever entered Narragansett Bay up to that time. Most of the immigrant passengers were Portuguese, with the greatest number having embarked at the Azores.[29]

In February 1912, D.H.G. Jones, an executive employed by James W. Elwell & Company, the line's American agents, addressed a gathering of important local personages and asked that two additional navigational lights be placed in Narragansett Bay for the safety of the company's vessels. He suggested that one be placed at Ohio Ledge (adjacent to Warwick Neck) and that the other be placed at North Point (at the northern end of Bristol's Poppasquash Point). If this were done, said Jones, the bay could be navigated "even without a pilot at night." He stated categorically that when the channel had been dredged to a uniform depth of thirty feet, the Fabre company would send its newest and largest vessels, the *Canada* and *Sant'Anna*, to Providence. Jones concluded by announcing that the Fabre Line would remain at the port as long as it was allowed to use the New Haven Railroad's wharf there. Jones's clear intimation was that if the railroad evicted the line, the lack of any other available facilities would force Fabre to quit Providence.[30]

Throughout this early period, Jones frequently demanded that the community provide the necessary facilities to handle cargo and that it furnish more comfortable accommodations for its passengers who disembarked at Providence. The New Haven Railroad prohibited the Fabre company from handling cargo at the wharf because of the interference and inconvenience this might cause with the railroad's own Long Island Sound steamers, which used the same docking area. The railroad had agreed only reluctantly and under pressure from the Providence community to allow the use of its wharf, the only such facility then available at Providence. The Fabre Line was the New Haven's unwanted tenant.

Twice the Fabre management issued explosive statements in the *Providence Journal* expressing dissatisfaction with the New Haven facilities. Adding force to this anger was Fabre's threat to leave Providence. The first controversy began when Bessie E. Bloom—head worker for the Immigrant Educational Bureau, an organization that aided immigrants upon their arrival at the port—wrote a letter to James W. Elwell & Company in New York. At this time, the company had no agents in Providence, so its American operations were directed from Elwell's New York office. Bloom's letter urged the line to improve the deplorable conditions under which immigrants were landed at Providence, especially with the winter approaching. The letter, apparently written sometime in early September 1912, specifically asked the line to install a "heating plant" in the shed on the New Haven–owned wharf at Fox Point.

In a response later that month, D.H.G. Jones agreed that conditions at the port were unsatisfactory, and he declared that Fabre might quit Providence unless certain of its demands were met, either by the railroad or by the community. These demands included the provision of adequate facilities at the port for the handling of cargo consigned to local merchants, as well as the provision of more humane and comfortable accommodations for the disembarkation of immigrants—accommodations that would eliminate the congested conditions at the old shed on the New Haven wharf where immigrants' baggage was inspected by customs officials. Jones maintained that only a small investment (he suggested $350.00) would be necessary to effectuate these improvements. However, "on principle," the Fabre Line did not care to make that expenditure, he said. If the state, the city or the railroad financed the improvements, the steamship company would continue to call at Providence. Jones pointed out that the New Haven Railroad was charging the Fabre Line $0.25 for each immigrant landed at its terminus. In view of conditions prevailing at the pier, he believed that this charge was unjust.[31]

With the New Haven apparently fearing blame if Fabre decided to abandon Providence, the local superintendent of the New Haven Company, J.A. Drooge, stated that he would do all that he could to induce the railroad to put its shed in satisfactory order. He said that the railroad had no opposition to installing a stove at the shed on the old Neptune Line wharf (as its wharf was then called) and that he would attempt to persuade the New Haven to lease additional space to the steamship line if the shed still proved to be inadequate and the state was willing to build an addition to the building. Drooge also asserted that he would recommend that a minimal fee be charged for use of the railroad's facilities. The New Haven Railroad, which was then unpopular because of its aggressive, monopolistic actions, could not simply relocate as the steamship company could, and it was definitely being badgered by the Fabre agents.

The superintendent pointedly defended the railroad, disclosing that Fabre had been permitted to use the New Haven's wharf free of any charge for a whole year, although this posed considerable inconvenience to the railroad's own maritime interests. With the New Haven company now levying a charge of $0.25 per immigrant arrival, the Fabre Line was paying between $25.00 and $50.00 per call, but never more than $100.00—an inconsequential amount. There were numerous occasions when the railroad's steamboats were delayed because a Fabre vessel was docked at its pier, said Drooge, and on some occasions, New Haven's freight was damaged.[32] There was no doubt that the railroad would prefer to be rid of the Fabre Line, but fear of popular opprobrium prevented the New Haven from ousting its demanding tenant.

At this time, the Fabre Line's unquestioning support from the *Providence Journal* was beginning to wane. In September 1912, the newspaper gave the following account:

> *On the surface of conditions as observed at the Fox Point wharf it would appear that the immigrants were obliged to undergo much hardship during the cold months. However, in so far as their examinations by the immigration officials is* [sic] *concerned, this examination takes place on board the steam-heated ship. In other words the vessels are examination quarters. As to better freight accommodations, it is asserted that the new State dock, under process of construction will remedy the present lack of facilities.*[33]

One year later, the dispute flared a second time. On this occasion, one of the principals was Gabriel Guez, a director of the Fabre Line at Marseilles. During early October 1913, Guez announced that unless the immigrant shed at the new state pier, then under construction, was made ready for the line's use by December 1, the company would quit Providence for the ensuing winter and perhaps permanently. "The winter is coming on," he said, yet where is "the immigrant shed on the new State wharf—where is that one facility so important to us for the comfort and protection of our passengers? Briefly, if we cannot be assured that it is to be completed by Dec. 1, we shall be obliged to cancel our service here."[34]

The director was further concerned with the facilities for handling freight, the depth of the existing channel and the railroad connections between the new state pier and the New Haven's planned main line. He reported that the propeller flanges and hulls of the company's steamers had been scraped in the port's shallow channel. Nevertheless, he asserted, "We would prefer to come to Providence, after our two years here, [and we] would like to develop the freight business, for we have six freight boats as well as seven passenger boats." Guez disclosed that other cities—Boston, Philadelphia and New Haven—"all with good facilities, or willing and anxious to provide them," had made attractive offers to the Fabre Line.[35]

Guez received the full support of the Providence Board of Trade, which said that the improvements then in progress at Providence Harbor were mere "flea bites" compared to what must be done to make the port what the board thought it should be. Figures were presented showing the amount of money invested recently by the port of Boston and the returns that ensued. The board urged the community to expend "millions of dollars" to make Providence a first-class harbor. The State Harbor Improvement Commission announced that a contract for an immigrant shed at the new facility had already been awarded and that the other matters alluded to by Guez would be attended to shortly.[36]

The Fabre agents attacked the New Haven Railroad in the press a few days later. Evidently coached by D.H.G. Jones, Guez called the New Haven's per capita landing fee of twenty-five cents "unreasonable" and demanded that the railroad charge a "frontage" fee instead. To reinforce its demands, the Fabre Line scheduled Boston for three calls between October and December 1913.[37] This pattern of making demands and then applying pressure was standard practice for the company.

In October 1913, shortly after the outburst by Guez, representatives of the Fabre Line, the New Haven Railroad, the City of Providence and the State of Rhode Island met in conference to address these recurrent problems. At this gathering, the differences among the principals were ironed out. The railroad agreed to make the necessary accommodations for passengers until the state pier was ready and, further, to make every effort to accommodate the line at the new dock with rail connections. Jones gave the signal that the crisis had passed by announcing that the line would remain in Providence. Perhaps the Fabre Line's honeymoon period at Providence had come to an end. A *Journal* editorial a week later said that the initial enthusiasm for the line had now been replaced by "an indifferent public sentiment regarding the line's establishment and continuance."[38]

One doubts the Fabre management's concern for the comfort afforded immigrants at the New Haven shed at Fox Point when the general condition of accommodations on steamship lines for steerage passengers is examined. Numerous histories of this traffic disclose that few of the immigrant lines cared much about the comfort of their poorer passengers. The Fabre Line was no different from the other transatlantic companies engaged in this service. During these early years, Fabre acquired the facilities it wanted by threatening to end its operations at Providence and by exploiting the community's desire to develop the port. One is left with the impression of a company that badgered both the community and the New Haven Railroad and exhibited an essential ingratitude for the services it received. The conflict with the New Haven, the city and the state was wholly unnecessary, inasmuch as the state pier, equipped with all the modern conveniences, was only two months from completion.

After a month of negotiations, state officials announced on November 7, 1913, that an agreement had been reached by the concerned parties with respect to the use of State Pier Number 1. The compact stipulated that the Fabre Line was to have a six-year lease of the south side of the dock, with the option to renew for four more years. The steamship company was to have "preferential" but not "exclusive" use of the wharf. The Fabre Line guaranteed the state a minimal yearly rental fee of $1,000. The agreement was signed in early November 1913.[39]

The new pier received its first ship on December 17, 1913, when the Fabre Line steamer *Venezia* docked. However, the *Venezia* was unable to land cargo because of an error in loading at Marseilles—the Providence-bound

This sketch was drawn by the engineer of the State Harbor Improvement Commission in January 1912 as construction began at State Pier Number 1. The panorama of the Providence waterfront along Allens Avenue depicts several landmarks, only one of which survives—the Providence Gas Company's purifier plant (now Conley's Wharf). It is the barrel-roofed structure along the shore at the left center of the rendering. *Conley Collection.*

IMMIGRATION TO RHODE ISLAND

This photo shows the steel-and-wood building at State Pier Number 1 shortly after its formal dedication on May 21, 1914. By that date, the dock had already experienced twelve arrivals. This building was six hundred feet long and one hundred feet wide and had two levels. The pier could accommodate two large ocean liners simultaneously. The south side was reserved under lease for the use of the Fabre Line. This image shows a bay steamer docked on the pier's north side. The structure was destroyed by fire on February 25, 1931. *Photo courtesy of the* Providence Journal.

Fittingly, Rhode Island's first Franco-American governor, Aram J. Pothier of Woonsocket, presided over the ceremonies dedicating State Pier Number 1 in May 1914. The popular Republican governor, a native of the province of Quebec, served as Rhode Island's chief magistrate from 1909 to 1915 and again from 1925 to February 3, 1928, when he died in office. His background and ethnicity influenced his supportive stance toward the Fabre Line. *Photo courtesy of the Rhode Island Heritage Hall of Fame.*

cargo had been wrongly stowed in the lowest portion of the vessel's hold. Despite this problem, the *Venezia* was met at the pier by a crowd of over two hundred people. The line entertained fifty of the more important onlookers aboard the steamer. It was not until June 1914, however, that the first cargo would successfully arrive at Providence via the Fabre Line.[40]

State Pier Number 1, as it was officially titled, was 600 feet in length and able to accommodate two large ocean liners at the same time. On the pier was a steel shed, 600 feet long and 100 feet wide, consisting of two stories. The wharf was later connected by spur tracks with the New Haven Railroad. The property adjacent to the dock, also owned by the state, fronted 700 feet on the river and contained a total of 748,523 square feet.

This facility was located on the west shore of the harbor equidistant between the Point Street Bridge to the north and Harbor Junction on the south. The front of the edifice was occupied by a fine suite of offices. The sides of the building were constructed so that any section or number of

A well-dressed and sizable group of local dignitaries were present on December 17, 1913, to welcome the *Venezia*, the first Fabre liner to dock at State Pier Number 1. Looking on from the deck above are hundreds of Italian and Portuguese immigrants waiting to debark. This six-year-old English-built vessel had accommodations for 80 first-class, 60 second-class and 1,800 third-class passengers. In October 1919, while chartered by Fabre to the French Line for its Cuba and Mexico service, the *Venezia* was destroyed by fire in the North Atlantic. *Photo by William Mills & Son, courtesy of the Rhode Island Historical Society.*

Immigration to Rhode Island

This is the most famous and reproduced photo of the Fabre Line and its immigrant arrivals. Here, they leave the *Venezia* clothed in their traditional southern European garb on this brisk mid-December day in 1913. *Conley Collection.*

sections between the piers and the frame could be readily hoisted and folded out to accommodate gangplanks from any part of the steamers. The lower floor of the structure was to be used for handling cargo; the second story was reserved for passenger examinations and processing.[41]

In the months that followed the opening of State Pier Number 1, the Fabre Line again requested that lights be placed at Ohio Ledge and North Point. This time it added No Man's Land (off Gay Head, Martha's Vineyard) to the list of places where it wanted improvements made. The Fabre steamer *Roma* had scraped its bottom on the dangerous shoals near that island and sustained damage to its hull plating during a passage on February 17, 1914, prior to a call at Providence. Adding difficulty to this unfortunate event, the steamer had 168 passengers on board who would have to be detained for ten days because of the existence of a single case of typhus fever. Because Providence did not as yet have a quarantine station and because the local steamship inspector was reluctant to allow the vessel to proceed with its passengers to New York, the *Roma* was threatened with a ten-day stay at Providence. Fabre agents appealed to local leaders for help, and accommodations were made to handle those quarantined at Providence. However, the *Roma* remained in Providence until April before proceeding to New York to have seventy-eight of its port hull plates replaced. The line had hoped to sail on to New York with only its crew on board, so it is puzzling why it remained at Providence for so long after its passengers were discharged. As usual, the Fabre company threatened to take its business elsewhere unless the community accommodated the quarantined passengers and provided adequate quarantine facilities sufficient to meet a similar contingency in the future.[42]

Providence mayor Joseph H. Gainer, an attorney by profession, was present at State Pier Number 1 both to welcome the *Venezia* in December 1913 and to formally open the facility in the following May. Throughout his long tenure—1913 to 1927—this very popular Democratic mayor lent his influential support to various efforts to make this transatlantic venture a success. *Photo courtesy of the Providence City Archives.*

Between May 1911 and July 1914, the Fabre Line made seventy-nine westbound passages and fifty eastbound passages that included calls at Providence. The steamship company carried over thirty thousand passengers to Providence, most of them classified as immigrant aliens, and it carried away over eight thousand.[43]

The Rhode Island delegation to Congress worked diligently during the spring of 1914 to have certain bills passed pertaining to the port of Providence. Among those considered was legislation that would make Providence an "immediate transportation port," allowing goods destined for other parts of the country to proceed immediately in bond from the port. Other proposed legislation sought money for equipping an inspection station at the state pier that would provide separate detention rooms for males and females. Congressman George F. O'Shaunessy, a native of County Galway, Ireland, worked for an appropriation of $25,000 to convert the old cruiser *Newark*, transferred from the navy to the Immigration Bureau, into a quarantine station.[44]

In early June 1914, Fabre's New York agent, the Elwell Company, suggested to the Providence Chamber of Commerce that sightseeing cars

THE PROVIDENCE JOURNAL, FRIDAY, MARCH 6, 1914.

TWO OCEAN STEAMSHIPS ARRIVE IN HARBOR IN ONE DAY.—FIRST TIME IN HISTORY OF PORT

This March 6, 1914 *Providence Journal* photo captures a memorable event in Fabre Line history: the first arrival at Providence of two liners on the same day. The *Madonna* is docked as the *Germania* cruises in midchannel to the south side of State Pier Number 1. Less than six months later, with Germany and France at war, that vessel's name was abruptly changed to *Britannia*. The *Germania/Britannia* was a ship of 5,103 gross tons, with a length of 410 feet. It had accommodations for 54 first-class and 1,400 third-class, or steerage, passengers. In one of the many ironies of history, the French built this ship in 1902 for the Fabre Line, which named it for Germany, a nation that became France's mortal enemy a dozen years later. Fabre then renamed the liner for Britain, which had been France's mortal enemy throughout the eighteenth and early nineteenth century. Today, all these countries are cooperating members of the European Union. *Photo courtesy of the* Providence Journal.

should be made available to take the line's first-cabin passengers on a tour of the city while the ships were at the dock discharging their cargos. Since most of the line's first-cabin passengers disembarked at New York, Elwell told the chamber that this tour would be an excellent way to advertise the merits of Providence to important people in the business world—people who might be looking for a favorable place to relocate or expand their businesses.[45] Probably Fabre was simply looking for a way to entertain its first-class passengers at no cost to the line while its steamers were discharging cargo.

Aboard the Fabre Line to Providence

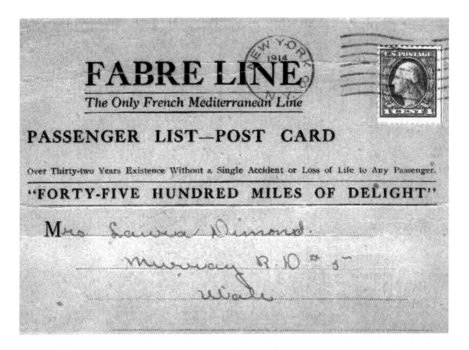

This Fabre Line postcard, mailed from New York in 1914, boasted that the company had operated "over thirty-two years without a single accident or loss of life to any passenger." Fabre did not mention a fire aboard the first *Alesia* on a voyage from Palermo to New Orleans in May 1899 that killed the ship's cook. Generally, the line's peacetime safety record was maintained until May 1930, when the *Asia* was destroyed by fire in the Red Sea while taking Muslims to Mecca, with the loss of about one hundred lives. *Conley Collection.*

GOFF & PAGE

Customs Brokers and Ship Agents

Order Your Goods Shipped—"*In Bond to Providence*"

224 Industrial Trust Building

In 1872, Henry Goff, a former U.S. customs agent, founded the Providence company of Goff & Page, a port facilitation firm that became the local agent for the Fabre Line. Former company president Norton W. Nelson has provided the authors with eyewitness information on the line's operation. Unfortunately, however, this extant firm has not retained the records of its transactions with the Fabre Line. *Providence City Directory.*

> 342   JANUARY SESSION, 1914—CHAPTER 1078.
>
> CHAPTER 1078.
>
> *Approved May 6, 1914.*
>
> AN ACT ESTABLISHING A COMMISSION TO INQUIRE INTO THE CONDITION, WELFARE AND INDUSTRIAL OPPORTUNITIES OF IMMIGRANTS AND ALIENS IN THE STATE OF RHODE ISLAND.
>
> *It is enacted by the General Assembly as follows:*
>
> *Commission on immigration, how appointed; powers and duties of.*
>
> SECTION 1. The governor is hereby empowered to appoint a commission on immigration, which shall consist of five members who shall serve without compensation, and which shall make full inquiry, examination and investigation of the status and general condition of immigrants and aliens within the state, including their way of living, distribution, occupation, educational opportunities and business opportunities and facilities, and also their relation to the industrial, social and economic condition of all the people of the state. The investigations of the commission shall be made with a view to obtaining information for the enactment of such laws as will bring non-English speaking foreigners, resident and transient, into sympathetic relation with American institutions and customs. For this purpose, said commission is hereby authorized to send for persons and papers, administer oaths and to examine witnesses and papers respecting all matters pertaining to this subject: *Provided*, that the state of Rhode Island shall not be subject to any expense in carrying out the foregoing purposes. Said commission shall make a full and final report to the governor, including such recommendations for legislation as in its judgment may seem proper, on or before January 15, 1915.
>
> *To make report on or before January 15, 1915.*
>
> SEC. 2. This act shall take effect upon its passage.

In May 1914, the general assembly, prompted by the influx of alien immigrants into Rhode Island via the Fabre Line, established a five-member state commission to report on their "way of living, distribution, occupation, educational opportunities, and business opportunities and facilities, and also their relation to the industrial, social, and economic condition of all the people of the state." This legislation was much more benign than the laws relating to immigrants enacted after World War I, because this commission lacked enforcement powers. *Public Laws of Rhode Island, 1914.*

During the early summer of 1914, the Fabre Line sent a circular letter to its European patrons announcing that except in cases of extreme haste, cargo could be transported to America more cheaply via the port of Providence than via New York.[46] Apparently, the company was satisfied with its New England port and was intent on transferring a larger share of its operations there. But the possibility of Providence's becoming a coequal terminus with New York was strongly and bluntly discounted by D.H.G. Jones, who told customs broker Frank A. Page of Goff & Page, Fabre's newly appointed Providence agent, that such an eventuality was a mere "dream." Jones said that he did "not believe that Providence could furnish sufficient business to make that a possibility," although he wished that it could.[47] It is unlikely that Jones, as an official of New York's Elwell & Company, a firm founded there in 1821, really wished that the port of Providence could generate sufficient Fabre Line business to become coequal with the port of New York, whose interest his company would naturally favor.[48]

The Fabre Line nonetheless entertained high hopes for the port of Providence and its business there; but then, in August 1914, the world was suddenly plunged into a terrible catastrophe—World War I began.

CHAPTER 3

DISRUPTIONS OF WAR

1914–1918

In early August 1914, Europe became entangled in a terrible war, a calamity that lasted until November 11, 1918. During this time, the Fabre Line saw its passenger traffic reduced to a mere trickle. By July 1915, only the *Roma* was calling at the port of Providence, making the complete voyage about once every two months. Except for one visit of the *Roma* on April 21, 1918, Fabre completely suspended sailings to the port after December 1917. Other steamship companies in the countries at war were experiencing the same hardships. Normal conditions were not restored between the Fabre Line and the port of Providence until the spring of 1919. The operations of the line during these war years reflected the general maritime reaction to the German menace on the high seas, especially the *unterseeboot*, or U-boat, as it is commonly called.

Archduke Francis Ferdinand, nephew of Emperor Francis Joseph and heir apparent to the thrones of Austria and Hungary, was assassinated along with his wife in the Bosnian city of Sarajevo on June 28, 1914. Exactly one month later, Austria-Hungary declared war on Serbia, believing that this act of violence by a Serbian nationalist required a strong response or it would threaten the monarchy's very existence. The assassination triggered a chain of events that culminated in World War I. By August 4, 1914, all the major powers of the continent were at war. The United States eventually entered the conflict in April 1917, and the world was never again the same.

On August 3, 1914, as the powers of Europe prepared for war, the newest and largest of the Fabre Liners, the *Providence*, was being launched at the

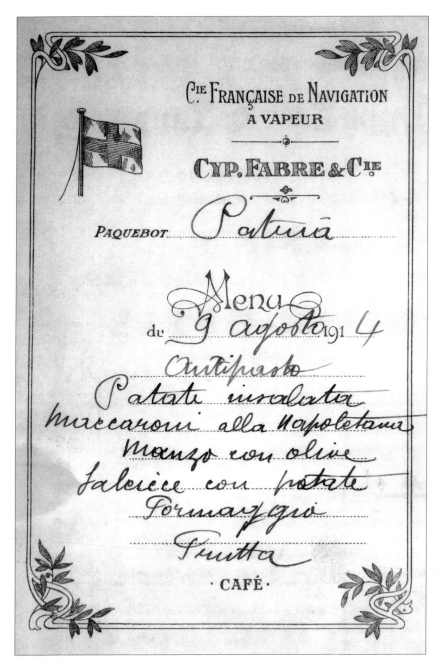

This dinner menu of August 9, 1914, was served to New York–bound first-class travelers aboard the *Patria* six days after Germany declared war on France. Italian cuisine, rather than French, was the choice of the ship's chef and reflected the nationality of the *Patria*'s passengers who had boarded at Naples and Palermo for the journey to America. *Conley Collection.*

government shipyard in Toulon near Marseilles. Like its sister vessels *Canada*, *Sant'Anna* and *Patria*, the *Providence* had been subsidized by the French navy, even though it was not fitted out completely until after the war.

The launching was to have been a joyous occasion. The naming of the vessel that was soon to become the queen of Fabre's fleet reflected the improving relations between the Fabre Line and the city of Providence. The original intention of the company was to christen the new steamer *Gallia*, a traditional Fabre name, but Mariano Vervena, the Italian consular agent at Providence, seconded by the city's chamber of commerce, suggested that the vessel be named for its intended American port of entry. After announcing that the vessel would be called *Providencia*, the company later decided to part with the thirty-five-year tradition of using Roman nomenclature and call it *Providence*.

Rhode Island's Franco-American governor, Aram J. Pothier, requested that the new ship be christened by Mrs. Samuel M. Conant, the wife of the chairman of the three-member State Harbor Improvement Commission, and the steamship company granted this request. Because the vessel was still under construction at the outbreak of the war, there was only an interim ceremony, although the line presented Mrs. Conant with a solid silver hatchet to be used eventually to sever the last strand tying the *Providence* to the ways. On one side of the hatchet was the coat of arms of the port of Marseilles, and on the other side was inscribed the following: "Fabre Line to Mrs. S.M. Conant, Providence, Aug 3, 1914."[49] Work on the *Providence* would remain incomplete until after the 1918 armistice ending the war, at which time the vessel would be refitted and make its maiden voyage to the port for which it was named. The *Providence* was the largest of the Fabre fleet, having a gross tonnage of 11,900 and a waterline length of 489 feet.[50]

Immediately after the war began, the fears of Allied steamship companies were directed more toward the seizure of their vessels by regular and auxiliary cruisers of the German navy than toward the torpedoing of them by German U-boats. The submarine was not feared by any of the steamship companies until after February 1915, when Germany stepped up its attacks on neutral commerce. Germany's U-boat fleet was at first assigned the role as scouts for the Imperial navy. Initially, the Germans did not expect to win the war at sea; they expected the decision to come quickly by land.[51] Enemy cruisers were the Fabre Line's most feared threat during the early months of the war.

Upon receiving the news that war with Germany and its allies was imminent, the Fabre Line, like the other transatlantic steamship companies, canceled all sailings and followed a "wait and see" policy. Its steamer

Aboard the Fabre Line to Providence

Sant'Anna, which was already at sea, was summoned back to port by a wireless command. Again, this action was in accord with the policy followed by the other transatlantic lines.

Perhaps the most noted return sailing was that of the German ship *Kronprinzessin Cecilie*. When the vacationists at Bar Harbor, Maine, awoke one morning during early August 1914, they were startled to observe the big North German Lloyd liner placidly anchored outside the yachts in Frenchman's Bay. One writer described what happened as follows:

> *Four days out of New York, Captain Charles Polack heard by wireless that war was imminent; he was also advised that two French cruisers were steaming to intercept him. Without a moment's hesitation or advice to his passengers, he turned the ship about... The men were asked to assemble in the smoking room. There they were informed that the ship was headed back to America. As* [the captain] *spoke, the stewards were extinguishing all lights on the ship. Some groped their way below to spread the news to their families while others stayed in the blacked-out smoking room for the night.*[52]

Less than two weeks after the war's outbreak, the Fabre Line steamship with the ironic name *Germania* entered Providence Harbor after an eighteen-day cruise that included changes in its course to avoid German naval vessels and threat of munity by its frightened crew. The *Journal* graphically reported the *Germania*'s passage, which is quoted here at length to give the reader a detailed contemporary account of the perils and apprehensions associated with merchant traffic on the high seas during World War I:

> *Leaving Marseilles on July 28, after several delays, the* Germania *shaped her course for Lisbon, where a large number of passengers were booked for New York. Even then it was not definitely known whether or not the ship would start across the Atlantic. The conflicting news did not tend to lessen the fears of the passengers, and it was not until several ships of the British and French Mediterranean squadrons were sighted that it was thought safe to pass out through Gibraltar and head north to the port of Lisbon. Although constantly in touch with the shore by means of the wireless, the captain and the officers did not divulge very much information for the benefit of the passengers, beyond reassuring them that they were in no danger. Every time smoke was sighted on the horizon meant a period of anxiety until it disappeared or the nationality of the vessel was discovered.*

Immigration to Rhode Island

At Lisbon all speed was made in embarking passengers and freight, and the Germania *cleared for the Azores on Aug. 2, arriving at St. Michael's Aug. 4, early in the morning. On the trip from Lisbon no warships and only a few merchant vessels were sighted, but in the Azorean port were 14 German merchantmen and several steamers carrying the Austrian flag, all held up awaiting orders from their owners.*

It was at the Azores that the members of the crew first learned of the seriousness of the situation in Europe. There were also vague rumors of the presence of a large number of German warships strewn out along the Atlantic coast of the United States waiting to prey upon any French or English vessels that happened along. As far as could be learned, the so-called mutiny of the vessel's crew at St. Michael's was inspired by two causes. Some thought that by leaving the Azores they were going into unnecessary dangers, and they did not relish the idea of being taken prisoners by any German warship. On the other hand, all were enthusiastic for the cause of France and were perfectly willing to have the ship put back for Marseilles, from which port they could join the colors.

The captain's orders were to proceed to Providence and New York, and orders were followed. Realizing that there was nothing really malicious in the attitude of the crew, the captain and his officers succeeded in making it plain to them that the men had shipped for the voyage and that they were bound to stand by the ship until it had reached its destination. He explained that he was in constant touch with the French warships and shore stations by wireless, and that he would not purposely take his ship into danger.

The news from Europe received at the Azores largely came from unreliable sources, little being official. While the Azores belong to Portugal, a neutral country, the majority of the islanders are in sympathy with the cause of France, and the most of the news made public there comes from French and English sources. It was common belief there that there were many German warships in American waters, notwithstanding the large number of German merchantmen in port, apparently afraid to put to sea. It was on Aug. 8 that orders came for the vessel to sail for Providence. The original date set for the sailing was Aug. 4. The reluctance of the crew had been overcome, and they appeared to be as glad as the passengers to be on their way to American waters.

Early in the morning on the second day out from St. Michael's smoke was reported off the starboard bow by the lookout. Capt. Ricordeau was immediately called and after a close examination through his glasses he decided to change his course. The sun was shining brightly, and by turning

> into the east and sailing in the direction with the distant ships he hoped to escape observation.
>
> During the previous night fragmentary wireless messages in the German code had been picked up which indicated the presence of German warships. When the smoke was sighted in the morning the captain decided to take no chances. By sailing at reduced speed during the day and covering all starboard lights at night the Germania was able to proceed on her way unmolested, and it is not thought that she was even sighted by the Germans.[53]

The passengers, crew and officers of the *Germania* breathed a sigh of relief when the vessel entered the safety of Narragansett Bay on August 15, 1914. "We are here and that is about all there is to say about it," the *Journal* quoted Captain Ricordeau as saying.[54] The *Germania* was simply completing a passage begun at the war's inception. By August 23, the Fabre Line had renamed the vessel *Britannia*, under orders from Marseilles demanding that immediate change.[55]

The Fabre Line bravely resumed service to New York in September 1914 and to Providence in October 1914. Visits continued at Providence through July 1915, after which only the *Roma* called at the port. That vessel averaged one round trip every two months until the spring of 1917, when its sailings became less frequent. Except for one visit in April 1918, there were none from December 1917 until April 1919, well after the war's conclusion. Fabre then began sending at least one vessel per month to Providence, and by February 1920, its sailings became much more frequent.[56]

The war-induced decline in passenger traffic reached its lowest ebb at Providence during 1919, when the total number of aliens admitted dropped to a mere 370 persons. This was in sharp contrast to the 12,103 alien arrivals in 1913 and the 10,822 who came in 1914, despite the outbreak of war. Out-migration on the line decreased after 1915, when 2,926 departed. A majority of those who did sail disembarked at Naples during the early years of the war, and a considerable number went to the Azores and to Lisbon. In 1918, there were no departures.[57]

In October 1914, Fabre announced that it intended to transport much of the freight from the Azores to America that was formerly carried to England and Germany by the ships of those nations.[58] Despite this announced change in policy, there was no appreciable increase in the cargo per call at the port of Providence. It seems unlikely that this change was ever implemented, unless the expected increase in cargo went on to New York instead.

Notwithstanding professed American neutrality, Mme. Emma Calve, "the celebrated 'Carmen' of the Grand Opries," performed in concert at the state pier for the benefit of the Allied wounded on January 8, 1915, after a cablegram asking permission to use the facility was sent from the Azores to Samuel M. Conant, chairman of the State Harbor Improvement Commission. Mme. Calve arrived on the *Venezia* on the day of the concert. About 1,200 people attended her performance, which raised $1,184 for its charitable purpose.[59]

By the time of this benefit concert, the facilities for handling immigrants at the port of Providence had apparently become superior to those at most of the other ports along the Atlantic Coast. In January 1915, Anthony Caminetti, U.S. commissioner general of immigration, proposed that Congress appropriate enough money to allow the federal Immigration Commission to take over the facilities needed for its work at the new State Pier because of its state-of-the-art condition.[60]

As Germany came to realize the strategic and economic potential of its U-boat fleet, it began its first U-boat offensive in February 1915 with operations in the North Sea and the waters adjacent to Great Britain. Germany was fighting for its life in this war, because the British had imposed a severe blockade on Germany that was causing much suffering and starvation among noncombatants. During the days of its initial U-boat offensive, from February 18 to September 20, 1915, the Germans destroyed a considerable amount of Allied tonnage. The most notable victim was the British liner *Lusitania*, sunk off Old Head of Kinsale, Ireland, on Friday, May 7, 1915, with the loss of 1,198 lives, 128 of whom were U.S. citizens. The big Cunard liner, loaded with ammunition to be used against Germany, was torpedoed at 2:10 p.m. and sank in eighteen minutes. According to recent historical research, the one torpedo that was fired caused an explosion of contraband in the forward hold of the vessel and blew out its bottom. As a consequence of American protests against this attack, German U-boat activity was suspended, because Germany then feared drawing America into the war on the side of Great Britain and its allies.[61]

The Fabre Line was apparently intimidated by the German announcement of submarine activities, because it scheduled no sailings to Providence during February 1915. Two of its ships, the *Sant'Anna* and the *Venezia*, were chartered to the Portuguese government during that month.

Aboard the Fabre Line to Providence

It also appears that the *Canada* had been commandeered by the French government.[62] While work on the *Providence* remained incomplete, the smaller and older vessels of the line, *Roma*, *Britannia* and *Madonna*, stayed in operation. In 1915, the French government announced that it had also drafted the *Britannia* and converted this ship into a transport for camels for use by the French army in its North African campaign.[63]

On the evening of September 12, 1915, the transmitting station at Cape Race, Newfoundland, picked up the following message from the Fabre Line ship *Sant'Anna*, which had sailed from New York four days earlier: "Steamer *Sant'Anna* in distress, on fire, in need of assistance. Position latitude 40':23" north; longitude 47'30" west."

The distress call was made because an explosion had occurred in one of the ship's hatches. Another explosion happened later. Fortunately, the fires were extinguished. The heat generated by the blasts had been great enough to warp the ship's plates. Amazingly, not a single life was lost, although 40 persons had been overcome by fumes. A total of 605 passengers from the *Sant'Anna* then proceeded under convoy with the *Ancona* to St. Michael's in the Azores, and shortly afterward, the vessel continued its passage to Naples.[64]

The fire aboard the *Sant'Anna* and suspicious occurrences at wharves in cities where the Fabre Line docked caused Elwell & Company to issue instructions to Goff & Page, the line's newly designated Providence agents, early in October: No one, except passengers, was to be allowed on the vessels when they were in port; friends of passengers were to be allowed on the pier only up to the foot of the gangplank; and proper passports were to be displayed. By mid-October 1915, the *Sant'Anna* had been requisitioned by the French government, converted for use as a hospital ship and sent to the Dardanelles, the strait between Europe and Asia near the Gallipoli Peninsula.[65]

The German government believed that Fabre Line vessels, as well as other transatlantic steamers belonging to the Allied nations, were carrying war materials to the Kaiser's enemies. Elwell's D.H.G. Jones emphatically denied the charge, stating that "the Fabre Line has not been carrying any arms or ammunition to ports in the Mediterranean touched by the steamers."[66] The Cunard Line had made a similar assertion, but in view of the historical analyses of the *Lusitania*'s sinking by Colin Simpson and Daniel Butler, one cannot take such an ex parte disclaimer as an unquestioned truth.[67]

After suspending their operations in the North Atlantic in September 1915, German submarines turned their attention toward the Mediterranean, so after that date, the sailings of the *Roma*—then the only Fabre vessel calling at Providence—originated from Barcelona, Gibraltar and Lisbon to avoid the increased danger posed by a departure from Marseilles or Naples. Many German U-boats were then based in the Adriatic Sea in waters controlled by Germany's ally Austria-Hungary and had easy access to the Mediterranean.[68]

Undaunted by the war in Europe, the Providence Chamber of Commerce attempted to enlarge the operations of the Fabre Line at the port of Providence. In early December 1915, the chamber sent a letter to the officers of the company at Marseilles suggesting that they route all possible Mediterranean cargo, both imports and exports, through Providence. The chamber suggested that Providence be designated as the American terminus for at least one of the Fabre steamers then operating, with others possibly added later "as the results warranted." The New Haven Railroad was to profit by this deal. Providence promoters attempted to enlist the support of the New Haven Railroad for the plan by asserting that the railroad would have a virtual monopoly at Providence. Even if the Southern New England, with its possible connection to the Canadian Grand Trunk, was to become a reality, it could not interfere with the New Haven Railroad's export business—or so urged the chamber. Both the New Haven and the Fabre Line could have a monopoly, if only each would give the plan a chance.

The chamber recommended that the Lisbon and Marseilles liners terminate at Providence. It conceded that Italian immigrants favored the port of New York, but other immigrant groups had definitely shown a preference for Providence. The Fabre Line could save $1,000 per day if its vessels did not need to proceed from Providence to New York. The chamber based its figures on a number of additional costs, including those of extra pilotage, general operations and the feeding of passengers and crew. In addition, observed the chamber, export rates from Pittsburgh and Cleveland, areas to which imported cargo could be shipped, were the same via Providence as they were via the port of New York.[69]

Fabre did not adopt the chamber's proposal. The *Roma*, after calling at Providence, continued on to New York for the remainder of the war years. The same Providence–New York westbound sailing pattern prevailed after the war ended, when the company placed its newest and largest vessels back in operation. However, it appears that these larger vessels called at Providence less often when they sailed eastward from New York during the 1920s.[70]

During the early months of 1916, Congress passed the Seaman's Act governing the operation of U.S. flag vessels. This legislation required that at least 75 percent of the seamen on a ship be able to take orders in the language of the officers and that 40 percent of the crew be able-bodied

Aboard the Fabre Line to Providence

Providence's contribution to the federal, state and local harbor revitalization project in the years 1909 to 1916 was the construction of a municipal wharf at Field's Point that was originally about three thousand feet long. This endeavor, the first of two major public works programs of the Gainer administration (the other being the expansion of the water supply system), was begun in 1914 and completed two years later. It involved the elimination of Field's Point and its famous public attractions in order to straighten the harbor line. It also included the laying of a spur track connecting the main line of the New York, New Haven & Hartford Railroad with the new docks. Mayor Gainer is shown in this November 1916 photo completing the project by driving a final golden railroad spike. *Photo from* Providence Magazine, *1916.*

seamen. Although of French registry and not subject to this legislation, the Fabre Line met the specifications of the law, at least with respect to the first provision, inasmuch as 90 percent of its crews were French.[71] It probably met the second specification as well. The law had been passed as a response to reports that torpedoed ships had experienced chaos during emergencies on board because of their proportion of Asian crew members who did not fully understand the orders of their officers. The Fabre Line certainly met the letter of the law; in this regard, its passengers were adequately protected.

Also in early 1916, the Germans initiated their second U-boat offensive in the North Atlantic. It continued unabated until March 1916, when Germany again suspended operations there as a consequence of American protests, although its U-boat activity continued in the Mediterranean. There, torpedo

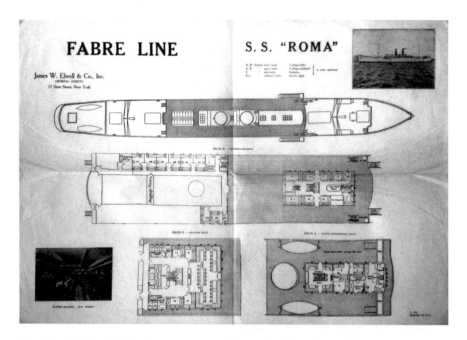

The *Roma*, built at the Mediterranean port of La Seyne, France, in 1902, was the workhorse of the Fabre Line fleet at Providence, recording seventy-six arrivals from September 9, 1911, to May 11, 1928, immediately after which it returned to its birthplace to be scrapped. A relatively small liner, the *Roma* was 411 feet long with a 46-foot beam. It had two funnels, two masts, a speed of fifteen knots and accommodated 54 first-class and 1,400 third-class passengers, as indicated here by its deck plan. *Conley Collection.*

attacks were quite severe, so the British rerouted their Australian and Far East commerce that formerly came through the Suez Canal to a passage around the Cape of Good Hope.[72]

Fabre vessels had their share of encounters with enemy warships and U-boats. The eastbound passage of the *Roma* in March 1916 from New York and Providence to Lisbon was fraught with special precautions taken to avoid being torpedoed. On this sailing, there seems to have been more than the usual fear of such an attack, perhaps because an attempt had been made to torpedo the *Patria* in the Mediterranean in early March 1916. The fired torpedo, seen by officers and passengers, missed the *Patria*'s stern by only thirty feet. The *Patria*'s captain at the time, Pierre Deschelles, said that the submarine had surfaced and then almost immediately submerged. The American consul general at Cairo, Rhode Islander Olney Arnold, told Captain Deschelles that he would make a full report of the incident to the U.S. government, but Arnold

Frank E. Fitzsimmons, the vigilant collector of customs for the port of Providence during the war years, was a prominent Democratic politician, serving as chairman of the Democratic State Committee from 1906 to 1914. He was especially active in war-related civic activities and soldier welfare and was the chairman of the committee that erected the seventy-five-foot-high World War I memorial monument near Market Square at the head of Providence's inner harbor at the junction of the Moshassuck and Woonasquatucket Rivers. *Photo from Charles Carroll,* Rhode Island: Three Centuries of Democracy.

died suddenly the day after the *Patria* reached Lisbon and before he could complete his report.[73]

On the passage to New York during the following month, the *Venezia*, three days out from Bordeaux, was attacked by two German merchantmen, or privateers, that had been converted into auxiliary cruisers. Three shots were fired at the Fabre steamer, but the vessel was in ballast and made an easy escape. At that time, the *Venezia* was being used as a freight carrier and had been chartered to another company.[74]

By the summer of 1916, Fabre vessels were carrying mounted guns, an innovation that gave customs collector Frank E. Fitzsimmons of the port of Providence a peculiar problem. The *Roma* had entered the port in July with a gun mounted on its stern, so the customs collector contacted Washington for instructions before allowing the armed ship to clear for New York. The *Roma*—which had sailed from Marseilles, making the first Fabre passage from that port in a year—was not held long at Providence, since the records indicate that the ship left on the same day that it entered the port, July 10, 1916.[75]

For the remainder of its wartime visitations, the *Roma* entered and cleared the port of Providence with a gun mounted boldly on its stern.

The effectiveness of such a defense is generally discounted by modern naval tacticians. The *Journal* reported that the *Roma* presented a "sinister" appearance upon entering the port on its passage from Lisbon and the Azores with every porthole covered and all its lights out. It was also mentioned that the steamer carried other deck guns, which in fact afforded it little defense against German torpedoes.[76] During most of the war, Fabre steamers were camouflaged.[77] They may even have been painted with dazzle stripes—a scheme then in vogue to confuse enemy U-boats about their sailing direction. After December 1917, as a consequence of the fierce submarine attacks and their influence on passenger traffic, the Fabre Line suspended all sailings until April 1919, except for a single visit from *Roma* in April 1918.[78]

The use of convoys minimized losses from German U-boat attacks and was instrumental in defeating Germany and its allies. Over a million American troops were landed in Europe during the war by convoy. No evidence has been found to suggest that the Fabre's *Roma* ever participated in a convoy. Convoys were in fact resisted for a good portion of the war by some lines, for many believed that vessels capable of sixteen knots or better were safer sailing alone. Although statistics proved that this concept was erroneous, the Fabre Line, which did not use convoys, managed to get through the war without too many losses on its various routes.[79]

During the conflict, many of the Fabre steamers were requisitioned by the French government to serve as hospital ships and to carry French colonial troops to the western front from North Africa. In 1914, the Fabre Line owned eleven ships, including eight passenger liners. The SS *Sant'Anna*, the vessel that had survived the suspicious September 1915 fire en route to Europe only to be requisitioned by the French government for military troop transport, was torpedoed in 1918 off Bizerte, Tunisia, with a loss of over five hundred lives. The SS *Libia*, *Provencia* and *Liberia* were the other three vessels lost by the company as a result of the conflict. None of these doomed ships ever docked at Providence. Two former Austrian ships, the *Braga* and the *Asia*, seized by the Brazilian navy as prizes of war, were purchased by the Fabre Line in 1920. Both of those vessels became familiar callers at Providence during the early 1920s.[80]

Although the *Roma* bore a distinctly Italian name, it did not bear many Italian immigrants to Providence during the war years because of the extreme hazards of Mediterranean travel. In 1915, 2,536 immigrants came to the port, followed by 4,029 in 1916, 5,070 in 1917 and 1,351 in 1918, as America became fully involved in the global conflict. Most of these arrivals hailed from continental Portugal or the Azores.[81]

Aboard the Fabre Line to Providence

The federal Literacy Test Act of February 1917 became another deterrent to immigration. Passed over the veto of President Woodrow Wilson, this measure required aliens over sixteen years of age to read "not less than 30 nor more than 80 words in ordinary use" in the English language or some other language or dialect. This act especially affected immigrants with humble backgrounds, most of whom lacked formal schooling and were illiterate. The act did not apply to aliens fleeing from religious persecution, nor did it prevent admissible aliens from bringing in illiterate members of their immediate families, but neither of these exceptions was of benefit to Providence's Portuguese migrants.[82]

On February 1, 1917, the Germans launched their third and final U-boat campaign in the waters around Great Britain and in the Mediterranean in a desperate all-out effort to win the war. They knew this policy of "unrestricted submarine warefare" would bring the United States into the conflict against them, but they believed that they could knock Great Britain out of the war before the United States could land a military force in Europe. Their actions in the North Sea were almost successful in starving Great Britain into submission, and the Germans might have achieved their goal had not the Allies begun to use ship convoys.[83] In response to this final, unrestricted U-boat effort, the Fabre Line announced in February 1917 that "owing to the present conditions" at sea, the *Roma* would omit its usual eastbound call at Providence, sailing directly from New York to Europe. However, by March 24, the persistent

Opposite: This detailed map of Providence Harbor was drawn by architectural historian John Hutchins Cady to reveal the dramatic progress of port development from 1909 to 1918. In the former year, a government-sponsored commercial survey declared that the port of New York was overburdened and advised steamship companies to divert some of their tonnage to other ports. Providence geared up to take advantage of the situation with the assistance of the state, which floated bonds in 1909 and 1912 to finance the acquisition of waterfront property in Providence, East Providence and Pawtucket. The state constructed State Pier Number 1, and the city built the municipal wharf. The federal government joined this partnership to upgrade the port, agreeing to match state and city expenditures, by dredging the entire harbor from Field's Point to Fox Point to a depth of thirty feet and a width of six hundred feet. The result of these improvements was dramatic. Providence became a major immigrant landing station, especially for Italians and Portuguese, and the city developed into a leading regional distributor of oil from the Gulf of Mexico area and lumber from the Pacific Northwest. The municipal pier, where Fabre ships docked from 1931 to 1934, is at the bottom of this map on the left, or west, bank; Fox Point, where the earliest Fabre vessels berthed, is at the top right; State Pier Number 1 is on the west bank about two-thirds of the way from the bottom of this drawing. *Sketch from John Hutchins Cady,* Civic and Architectural Development of Providence.

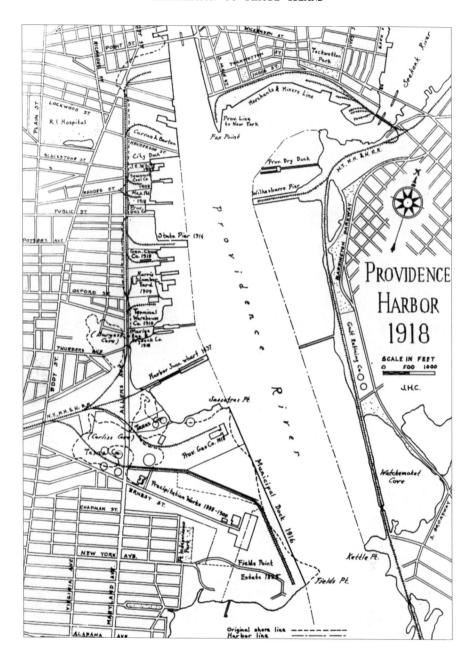

Roma was again making westbound calls at the port of Providence, and it made five additional visits between that date and war's end.[84]

On November 11, 1918, an armistice brought the First World War to a conclusion, with Germany forced to make an unconditional surrender, to assume full responsibility for the war and to pay punitive financial reparations to the Allied nations. With the war over, but with the seeds of another global conflict unwittingly sown, Fabre gradually set about regaining its prewar business and expanding its operations at the port of Providence.

CHAPTER 4

REVIVAL AND REPRESSION

1919–1921

World War I adversely impacted not only immigration to America but also America's attitude toward foreign immigrants. Traumatized by the carnage of World War I and the devastating influenza pandemic of 1918–19, America's mood was fearful and suspicious. We were allegedly the victors in President Woodrow Wilson's self-proclaimed war "to make the world safe for Democracy," yet many Americans of the hyphenated kind—especially Germans, Irish and Italians—had been less than unanimous in supporting a war in concert with our English and French allies.

In 1917, as America entered the conflict, Russia withdrew and was soon in the grip of the Bolsheviks. These communist ideologues preached world revolution and the overthrow of capitalism. In 1919, their American sympathizers established the Workers' (later the Communist) Party in the United States. Simultaneously, the massive wave of immigration that had crested in the decade prior to World War I began to surge again. Slavs, Jews, Greeks, Arabs, Portuguese, Italians and other foreign language–speaking arrivals were perceived by some as a threat to American values and culture, since a few of these immigrants even preached anarchism.

These conditions spawned a movement styled by its advocates as "100 percent Americanism." This was a creed that regarded alien tongues, thoughts and customs as inferior, suspicious and subversive.

Rhode Island was not immune to this cultural paranoia. The rural, old-stock politicians in control of the powerful legislature regarded the

Aboard the Fabre Line to Providence

When the war ended, Providence was visited by a series of Allied heroes, including Cardinal Desideratus Mercier, primate of Belgium, and Marshal Ferdinand Foch, commander of the Allied forces in Europe. Not to be outdone, Italy sent Generalissimo Armando Vittorio Diaz (shown here), whose army crossed the Alps to force the surrender of Austria-Hungary. At the left in this photo, taken on the steps of city hall, is Colonel G. Edward Buxton, a prominent Rhode Island military figure; at the right in this image is Italian vice-consul Mariano Vervena, principal local promoter of the Fabre Line. *Photo from David Patten*, Rhode Island Story.

urban ethnic groups as people much in need of social control. If these new arrivals could not be deported, at least they could be homogenized, melted, domesticated and rendered less of a menace to American values.[85]

In May 1914, the general assembly had established a commission "to inquire into the condition, welfare and industrial opportunities of immigrants and aliens in Rhode Island." This five-member board was unpaid and had no expense account. It was to make "a full and final report to the governor, including such recommendations for legislation as in its judgment may seem proper" by January 15, 1915. A year later, this body was given a one-year extension to file its report. What legislation (if any) emanated from its deliberation is unknown to us. The commission expired in 1920.[86]

Meanwhile, on April 24, 1919, the Rhode Island legislature passed two "patriot acts" to promote 100 percent Americanism and combat the so-called hyphenated Americanism that caused immigrants to be preoccupied with developments in their homeland or to espouse a radical ideology. One statute was appropriately entitled "An Act to Promote Americanization." It was solely language oriented, but it brought the melting pot to a boil. The law directed local school committees "of every town in which twenty or more persons more than sixteen and less than twenty-one years of age who cannot speak, read, and write the English language are resident" to establish evening schools for the purpose of educating such illiterates. The school committees also had the option of establishing day schools for the same purpose.

IMMIGRATION TO RHODE ISLAND

CHAPTER 1802.

AN ACT TO PROMOTE AMERICANIZATION.

It is enacted by the General Assembly as follows:

SECTION 1. One or more public evening schools, in which attendance shall be free for persons resident in the town in which such school shall be located, and in which the speaking, reading and writing of the English language shall be taught for two hours on each of at least one hundred nights between the first of September and the first of June in each year, shall be established and maintained by the school committee of every town in which twenty or more persons more than sixteen and less than twenty-one years of age who cannot speak, read and write the English language are resident; *Provided,* that the school committee of two adjoining towns may unite for the purpose of establishing and maintaining jointly, at some convenient place, an evening school for persons resident in both towns.

SEC. 2. The school committee of any town may establish and maintain one or more public day continuation schools for the teaching of the English language and American citizenship, at which any person beyond compulsory school age, resident in such town may attend free of expense, or may make provisions, at the expense of the town, for the attendance of such persons in continuation schools in other towns.

SEC. 3. Every person who has completed sixteen years of life and who has not completed twenty-one years of life, and who cannot speak, read and write the English language in accord with standards approved by the State Board of Education, and who resides in a town in which the school committee has established a day continuation school for the teaching of the English language, or an evening school, shall attend either the day continuation school or the evening school at least two hundred hours between the first day of September and the first day of June in every year until he shall have acquired reasonable facility in speaking, reading and writing the English language in accord with standards approved by the State Board of Education. For the purpose of this act day continuation or evening schools may be established in shops or factories, *Provided* that such schools are under control and supervision of the school committee. Attendance in private schools or private instruction in the English language may be accepted as compliance with this act in lieu of attendance on public instruction only if the private instruction is approved by the school committee as substantially equivalent in content, method and the hours of instruction to the instruction offered in public schools. Persons instructed in private schools or receiving private instruction in accordance with the provisions of this section shall be deemed as having acquired reasonable facility in speaking, reading and writing the English language as provided in this section, only after the successful passage by such person of an examination, provided for by the school committee.

SEC. 4. Any person who has completed sixteen years of life and who has not completed twenty-one years of life, and who does not speak, read and write English in accord with standards approved by the State Board of Education, who resides in a town in which the school committee has made provision for the teaching of the English language in compliance with this act, who habitually absents himself from public instruction, is sufficiently irregular to make it impossible for him to complete two hundred hours of instruction annually within the time set by the school committee for conducting such schools, and who is not attending private instruction approved by the school committee as provided in section 3 of this act, may be fined for each wilful absence one dollar and not exceeding twenty dollars in the aggregate during one year or for persistent refusal to attend such instruction, may be committed to an institution during his minority.

Rhode Island's April 1919 "Act to Promote Americanization" speaks for itself. It was inspired by the so-called hyphenated American opposition to American involvement in World War I, by the resumption of the "new" immigration, by the "Red Scare" and by the 100 percent American movement of that era. *Public Laws of Rhode Island, 1919.*

In these special schools, Americanization classes were taught for two hundred hours over at least one hundred days or evenings. The sessions were mandatory for the target group, and failure to attend regularly carried a fine of one dollar for each "willful absence" (weekly pay then ranged from eight to fourteen dollars). For "persistent refusal to attend such instruction," a truant could be "committed to an institution during his minority" (i.e., until he or she was twenty-one years old).

Classes such as this one at an East Side Providence school prepared immigrants for citizenship, even prior to the enactment of the harsh Americanization statute of 1919. This session, held around the time of the *Madonna*'s first arrival, depicts Molly Katz (right foreground) and her foreign-born classmates diligently absorbing a lesson in civics. Note the formal attire worn by these early twentieth-century students. *Photo courtesy of the* Providence Journal.

A companion measure was much more draconian. Entitled "An Act to Protect the Government of the State of Rhode Island and the Government of the United States of America," it outlawed various forms of protest and dissent. The most repressive provision of the statute (which still survives as Title 11, Chapter 43, Sections 11–14, of our General Laws) criminalized mere advocacy "of any change, alteration or modification in the form of government of the State of Rhode Island, except in the manner provided by the Constitution or the laws of the State of Rhode Island or by the Constitution or laws of the United States." Transgressors could be fined up to $10,000 and/or imprisoned for as long as ten years. Further, any meeting at which the acts proscribed by the act were "advocated, taught, or discussed" was declared to be "an unlawful assembly." Given the temper of the times and the conservatism of the courts, this law might then have survived a constitutional challenge.[87]

Immigration to Rhode Island

On May 26, 1919, armed with the new statute, Providence mayor Joseph Gainer and the Providence police commissioners announced the start of "a vigorous campaign" against Bolsheviks, members of the Industrial Workers of the World and "other radicals." The Rhode Island phase of the "the Great Red Scare" was in full swing. In July 1918, Socialist leader Joseph M. Coldwell of Providence had been convicted in federal court on a charge of "seditious libel" under the wartime Espionage Act. When the U.S. Supreme Court refused review in October, Coldwell was sent to a federal penitentiary to serve a three-year term.

The hunt for subversives reached its peak in early 1920. On January 2, federal agents in concert with Providence police stormed the abodes of known Socialists and arrested sixteen for alleged radicalism. Three days later, federal authorities seized "radical papers" from the Olneyville Square dental office of local Socialist leader Dr. James P. Reid. Meanwhile, the Providence Police Commission denied congressman and national Socialist Party leader Victor Berger and Irish labor organizer Big Jim Larkin ("the Lion of Irish Labor") permission to speak in Providence. Fabre Line arrivals from Russia received special scrutiny from immigration officials who were primed to detect those with Bolshevik sympathies.[88]

In sharp contrast to this wave of xenophobia, the Catholic Church, especially its ethnic parishes and their allied religious orders, as well as Orthodox churches and synagogues, came forward to welcome the immigrants, especially those of their particular faith. A citizens' group called the Union of Christian Work established an Immigrant Education Bureau to relieve the "acute suffering of women and children" at the dock, in the home and in the schools, while hopefully gaining converts to Protestantism.

Led by Prescott O. Clarke, this nominally "Christian" organization hired Bessie E. Bloom (later Bessie Wessel) as its "head worker." Bloom, a woman of Jewish faith, was a recent graduate of Brown University who later earned a doctorate in sociology and became an authority on American ethnic groups. Bloom's summary of her bureau's goals and methods was as follows:

> *The Immigrant Educational Bureau traces immigrant children to see that they come under the proper influences, conducts extensive lecture work which interests thousands of immigrants, reaches several hundred persons through its Library on Livingstone Street, conducts a Social Center at the Old Branch Avenue School, and is continually organizing new classes and bringing them in touch with Americanizing institutions. All steamers are*

met by workers speaking foreign languages, and a lunch counter is being conducted to expedite matters at the wharf.

In true ecumenical spirit, this Protestant organization employed a young Jewish female scholar to proselytize Catholic immigrants.

More civic than religious, the Legal Aid Society stepped in to assist the new arrivals in coping with the myriad of rules and regulations that they encountered in adjusting to life and work in America. The combined work of these churches and agencies would fill yet another book and is well beyond the scope of this mainly maritime history.[89]

Another salutary effort was the local response to the American Citizenship Campaign, in which Catholic clergy played a significant role. By February 1919, the campaign's workers had contacted over twenty thousand of the nearly forty-four thousand Rhode Island residents who had not applied for citizenship, and over five thousand became citizens as a result of this drive.[90]

In late January 1919, Elwell & Company announced that the Fabre Line would resume service between Providence and the Azores, Portugal and Mediterranean ports. Elwell expected that the French government would shortly be releasing commandeered vessels of the line.[91] The *Roma*, the only Fabre vessel that remained in operation during most of the war, had last docked at Providence in April 1918.

Before the war, the Fabre vessels that visited the port were the *Madonna*, *Germania* (aka *Britannia*), *Venezia* and *Roma*; after the war, the *Canada*, *Providence*, *Asia*, *Patria*, *Sinaia*, *Alesia* and *Braga* made regular calls at Providence, in addition to those made by some of the older vessels.[92]

Having initiated service in April 1919 with the arrival of the *Britannia*, Fabre scheduled no sailings in the following month.[93] It took the line some time before it was able to reestablish its old travel patterns and develop new ones.

On June 19, 1919, as the *Britannia* entered Narragansett Bay on its return passage from New York, fire broke out in the vessel's forward hold, probably caused by spontaneous combustion. The flames were contained by the crew with the aid of a steam hose until the vessel reached Providence. A city fire engine awaited the *Britannia*'s arrival at the state pier and extinguished the fire in short order by pouring a steady stream of salt water into the vessel's hold. Several tons of sugar that had been stowed in that hold were destroyed in the process; otherwise, the fire caused only minor damage. Having survived the mishap, the *Britannia* departed for the Azores and the Mediterranean that same day, carrying 168 passengers from New York and another 800 who boarded in Providence. The vessel also carried Dr. Albert Cousinery, a representative of the Fabre Line, who expressed thanks on behalf of the line to the Providence Fire Department for the prompt assistance it had rendered to the *Britannia*, which he called "a child of Providence."[94]

Dr. Cousinery was to bear a more important message to the Providence community than a mere thank-you. Addressing the Providence Chamber of Commerce at the Narragansett Hotel on the evening of his arrival, Cousinery reported that his company wanted to do all that it could to develop and increase Providence's local trade. He told the gathering:

> *The Fabre Line intends to help develop the port of Providence and to encourage shipping via Providence to European ports, as well as import trade to this city. The war and the commandeering of ships of the line by the French Government for use as troop transports and hospital ships had necessitated discontinuance of the service from this side of the Atlantic. The return of the ships now, with the cessation of war needs, has made possible the resumption of the contemplated expansion of the service.*

Cousinery further announced that the line intended to open an office at Providence and that it would have a representative there to arrange all the details relating to the sailing of its ships. Large steamers were also to come to the port as soon as business warranted. In sum, the Fabre Line wanted to expand its activities at Providence with regard to both cargo and passenger traffic. Implicit in the message was the challenge to the community to contribute to this effort.[95]

Finally, Cousinery expressed satisfaction that a dry dock was being constructed at the port—a facility that was reported to be the largest of its kind between New York and Boston.

Since construction had also begun the previous February on rail connections between the state pier and the New Haven Railroad, Cousinery suggested that when these facilities were completed, it might even be possible to load steamers entirely at Providence, without sailings having to originate at New York.[96] But this prospect never came to pass. The Fabre Line probably entertained little thought of eliminating calls at New York entirely under any circumstances because too much freight originated there. No doubt Dr. Cousinery had in mind the establishment of an independent Providence service direct to foreign ports.

George Holmes, a former member of the State Harbor Improvement Commission who had numerous dealings with the Fabre Line during its early years at the port, was not wholly enthusiastic about Dr. Cousinery's message.

"As a business venture," he told the Providence Chamber of Commerce, "the State of Rhode Island has not found the Fabre Line profitable to date. In the future, we will, I think, have to have some very definite assurances that the Fabre Line will make some sacrifices to develop the port of Providence." Holmes suggested that the line give its proposed Providence run a sufficient period of trial time to direct freight routes from Naples and Marseilles to Providence as evidence of its good faith. He predicted that increased tourist travel from Providence to Europe would follow if there were more sailings.[97]

The *Providence Journal* responded to Dr. Cousinery's statement with enthusiasm, certain that Fabre would be well assisted in developing export cargoes from New England via Providence. The newspaper proudly retorted, "Why not? In a word there is no harbor so attractive for future development as our own...Every citizen of Providence should rejoice in the promise of a continuation and increase of the Fabre service and in the hope that other important maritime connections will be expeditiously secured."[98]

Through a letter to the *Journal* in July, the Fabre Line announced that the *Canada*, one of the line's largest vessels, would sail from the Mediterranean to Providence and arrive in two weeks.[99] In response to Dr. Cousinery's implicit challenge and the announcement of the *Canada*'s projected arrival, the Providence Chamber of Commerce proposed educating western shippers about the advantages of sending their freight through Providence rather than through New York. Although rail rates were about equal to each of the two cities, Providence had the advantage of being free of congestion, a fact that the chamber believed was not known to distant exporters.[100] Once again, Providence seemed to be on the move.

When the *Canada* arrived on July 26, 1919, it struck bottom at the state pier, though it was drawing a mere twenty-two feet of water. The incident indicated that dredging was needed again. During the war years, the inactive harbor had apparently filled with mud from the outflow of the Seekonk, the Moshassuck and the Woonasquatucket, but this silting remained unknown to harbor authorities until it was revealed by the *Canada*'s mishap. Upon leaving the harbor, the vessel again stirred up mud from the channel bottom. Dredges attended to the problem shortly afterward.[101]

The Fabre Line secured a renewal of its lease on the south side of the state pier in November 1919. By the terms of the agreement, the line was to guarantee at least one sailing per month between Providence and the Azores, continental Portugal and the Mediterranean. The frequency of the sailings was to be increased to one every twenty days when business warranted. The financial part of the arrangement, which was not released until February 1920, stipulated that rental fees were to vary in accordance with business conditions, with a per capita tax on passengers, a dockage charge on vessels and a wharfage assessment on freight handled at the pier. The minimum annual rental fee was $5,000 instead of the $1,000 charged formerly. The new lease, covering a four-year period with a renewal option of six more years, again gave the line "preferential" treatment on the south side of the wharf.[102] During February 1920, the U.S. Army Corps of Engineers completed a thirty-foot channel that was to extend into Providence Harbor as far as the state pier. A twenty-five-foot channel existed at the time as far north as Fox Point.[103]

The problem of getting American businessmen to realize the opportunities to be had by shipping via the port of Providence remained foremost in the minds of officials at the chamber of commerce during 1920.[104] It was a problem that these business leaders were never able to solve. In June 1920, the Fabre Line reappointed Goff & Page as its local freight agents; Mariano Vervena, then president of the Columbus Exchange Bank, was chosen as its passenger agent.[105]

By the beginning of 1920, the Fabre Line had gained back much of its prewar business, especially with respect to immigrant traffic. These years between the end of the First World War and the imposition of the Emergency Quota Act of 1921—the first of two quotas to stem the new immigration from southern and eastern Europe—were boom years for the Fabre company. During this time, its passenger traffic soared to unprecedented heights. A major attempt was also made to expand freight traffic through the port of Providence by making the port Fabre's principal cargo-handling location in America, but this development did not materialize. The line reached its apogee at Providence in 1920, when immigrant arrivals totaled 12,860 and total passenger traffic reached 13,300.[106]

Considerable out-migration from the port occurred during the postwar years. Many in the Portuguese community had been anxiously awaiting the resumption of full Fabre service so that they might return to their native land to visit relatives. Other returnees were seasonal workers who came to Cape Cod and its environs each spring to pick cranberries and then departed for their native land in the fall months with the savings that they had amassed. Also awaiting return passage to their homeland were those Portuguese and Italians who could not remain in America because of their failure to meet the standards required by the Literacy Test Act of 1917. Most of these out-migrants from Providence disembarked at the Azores; Lisbon was the second most frequent port of debarkation. In 1920, this out-migration from Providence was at its all-time heaviest, with 5,249 departures.[107]

Aboard the Fabre Line to Providence

To assist with this return service, the line eventually appointed an agent at heavily Portuguese New Bedford. In colorful Portuguese-language posters, Guilherme M. Luiz and Company advertised trips (mostly outward bound from Providence) to the Azores, Cape Verde, Madeira and Lisbon.[108]

Christened at the outbreak of the war, the Fabre Line's largest and newest vessel, the 489-foot *Providence*, entered Narragansett Bay on its maiden voyage from the Mediterranean on June 17, 1920. A three-day reception followed, with the chamber of commerce presenting M. Paul Vernet, an administrator of the line, with a bronze tablet bearing the following inscription:

THIS TABLET IS
PRESENTED BY
THE CHAMBER OF
COMMERCE OF THE CITY OF
PROVIDENCE, RHODE ISLAND, U.S.A.
TO COMMEMORATE
THE FIRST ARRIVAL OF THE
FABRE LINE STEAMSHIP
PROVIDENCE
AT THE PORT FOR WHICH
SHE IS NAMED
JUNE MCMXX

The tablet was to be placed at the head of the vessel's grand stairway. The events that took place with the arrival of the *Providence* were similar to those at the first arrival of the *Madonna* in May 1911, when Fabre inaugurated service to the port. As the *Providence* passed Warwick Neck, whistles and sirens belched out their eerie cries. Fittingly enough, "Tal" Dodge piloted the big ship as it carried 2,150 passengers from Europe.[109]

Captains employed by the Fabre Line to command its vessels were capable at times of extraordinary seamanship. The *Britannia*, arriving at Providence on October 26, 1920, had encountered two severe storms on its passage from Europe. At one point, the ship had actually been on the rocks off one of the smaller islands of the Azores group, and only by superb navigation did its captain manage to get it free. The vessel sustained only slight damage to its hull

Opposite, bottom: City dignitaries and Fabre Line officials pose on the deck of the *Providence* following its arrival on June 19, 1920. *Photo courtesy of the* Providence Journal.

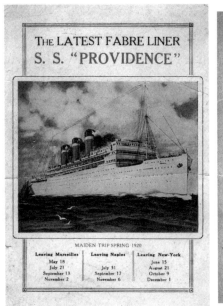
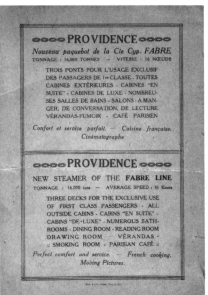

The SS *Providence* was formally launched on August 3, 1914, the day Germany and France went to war. The conflict delayed the maiden voyage of this queen of the Fabre Line until June 1920. As this flyer indicates, the vessel came to its namesake city with great fanfare. *Conley Collection.*

Aboard the Fabre Line to Providence

The SS *Providence* is depicted in this postcard as it arrives at the port of Providence. Most official ship registers record its gross tonnage as 11,900, but its maiden-voyage flyer incorrectly sets that figure at 16,000 tons. Built by Forges & Chantiers at LaSeyne, France, the vessel was 489 feet in length with a beam of 59.8 feet. It had accommodations for 140 first-class, 250 second-class and 1,850 third-class passengers. Its last visit to Rhode Island came on November 25, 1931. After more than three decades of additional Mediterranean service, the *Providence* was scrapped at LaSpezia, Italy, in 1951. *Conley Collection.*

and proceeded at a normal speed to Providence. About nine hundred miles off Nantucket, the *Britannia* encountered a second storm, which snapped off most of its rudder. Captain Laurent Vidal brought the steamer to the mouth of Narragansett Bay, where it was met by tugs that took it on the remainder of its journey to Providence. Upon reaching the port, many of the passengers praised Captain Videl's seamanship in statements to the press.[110]

The years following the First World War were good ones for the Fabre Line. More immigrants and total passengers were handled at Providence during 1920 and 1921 than during any other two-year period in the history of the line there. Most of this passenger traffic came from the Azores and Portugal. The Fabre Line made a total of thirty westbound and thirty-five eastbound sailings with calls at Providence from its resumption in April 1919 until July 1921.[111]

Passenger traffic sustained the Fabre company at Providence during these years as it had in earlier times, for the line was never able to develop enough cargo traffic through the port to forgo sailings to New York. Unfortunately,

Immigration to Rhode Island

The *Asia* (formerly known as *Alice*), shown here, and the *Braga* (formerly known as *Laura*) were sister ships of 6,122 gross tons built in Glascow, Scotland, in 1907 for the Austrian company Unione Austriaca of Trieste before the Austro-Hungarian Empire lost its outlet on the Adriatic Sea. During World War I, both the *Asia* and the *Braga* were seized by the Brazilian navy in retaliation for the sinkings of Brazilian cargo ships by German U-boats. Because Austria was Germany's ally, the Treaty of Versailles, ending the conflict, allowed Brazil to keep over seventy ships that it had seized from the Central powers. The *Asia* and the *Braga*, both part of this reparations fleet, were sold to the Fabre Line in 1920. Beginning with the visit of the *Asia* on October 5, 1920, both ships made numerous calls at Providence, but their closely shared histories included tragic endings: the *Braga* was shipwrecked and sunk in the Aegean Sea in November 1926, fortunately with no loss of life, and the *Asia* was destroyed by fire in the Red Sea in May 1930, with a loss of around one hundred lives, while carrying Muslim pilgrims to Mecca. *Photo courtesy of Heritage Ships.*

passenger traffic was severely affected during the following years by the congressional enactment of the discriminatory quota acts of 1921 and 1924. The legislation forced the line to extend its operations eastward in the Mediterranean in order to secure a sufficient number of passengers that would be eligible to enter the United States. Despite this blow to its operations, the company managed to sustain itself at Providence until the worldwide Great Depression of the 1930s forced it to end its sailings there forever.

CHAPTER 5

THE QUOTA YEARS

1921–1925

The Fabre Line faced formidable difficulties after July 1, 1921, the effective date of the Emergency Quota Act that had become law on May 19, 1921. It was the first of the two major immigration statutes of the decade. The other was the even more stringent National Origins Act of May 24, 1924. These restrictive laws were aimed at limiting the large number of immigrants who were coming to this country from southern and eastern Europe after the war. Americans believed at the time that these people—with cultural, linguistic, religious and ethnic backgrounds different from those of native-born Americans—could not be assimilated. The quota legislation passed during these years of "100 percent Americanism" continued in effect throughout the remainder of the Fabre Line's operations at Providence and onward until 1965.

The quota laws forced the line to look eastward in the Mediterranean for passengers. From this point on, Fabre's manifests displayed a more cosmopolitan complexion than they had during the line's earlier years at Providence. Fabre now made calls in North African, Middle Eastern, Aegean and Black Sea ports. Statistics indicate the severe decline of the line's immigrant traffic as well as its more heterogeneous ethnic nature. Fabre managed to survive at the port of Providence during these years, but its future there was precarious. Never again did the company carry as many passengers as it had prior to the institution of the quota system.

Until 1820, immigration to America had not been a major concern to native-born Americans, for although there had been a constant flow of Europeans to our shores, most of the newcomers reflected the earlier established ethnoreligious composition of the population. This immigration, generally termed "colonial" or "early," otherwise remains ethnically unclassified. These terms seem to reflect little of the concern about immigration that this issue would engender in future years.

European immigration between 1820 and 1882 has been called the "Old Immigration." During that time, America received many immigrants who came principally from Ireland, Germany, Scandinavia and Great Britain—northern and western Europe. Until the racially motivated exclusion of the Chinese in 1882, there were practically no restrictions on immigration.

The first general immigration law that affected transatlantic steamship companies was the so-called Passenger Act of August 1882. This act excluded criminals, paupers, the insane and other "undesirables" from entry into the United States. It further imposed a head tax of fifty cents on steamship companies for each immigrant landed. This tax was increased to two dollars in 1903 and to four dollars in 1907. Minor immigration laws had been passed previously, but as pro-restrictionist immigration historian Ray L. Garis noted in 1927, the Passenger Act of 1882 "was indeed a big important step forward—the first one of any real importance, either state or national."[112]

The Foran Act of February 1885 targeted another group of immigrants—contract laborers. This bipartisan measure, demanded by organized labor, made it unlawful "to assist or encourage the importation or migration of aliens…under contract or agreement…to perform labor or service of any kind in the United States." This legislation, directed mainly against potential strikebreakers, did not apply to the skilled labor needed for new industries nor artists, actors, lecturers, singers or domestic servants.[113]

Congress further regulated the flow of immigrants into the country at various times between 1885 and the First World War. The nativistic Garis sympathetically summarized this legislation as follows:

> *Throughout the development of this body of laws, well-marked tendencies can be traced. In the first place, the criteria of admission have steadily increased in severity, until in 1914 the law provided for the exclusion of virtually every undesirable class, with the probable exception of illiterates. In the second place, there is an increasing concentration of all business connected with immigration in the hands of a single branch of the Federal Government. Third, we find an increasing determination on the part of*

the United States to assert its right to protect itself against unwelcomed additions to its population, not only by refusing them admission, but by expelling them from the country when we deem it expedient for our own welfare. It is evident from the laws themselves that bar after bar was put up as time went on. Not once have we found a provision which let down a single bar once it had been put up. Although the early efforts were largely futile, the laws brief, and the machinery inadequate, yet progress was rapid, so that by 1914 we were in a position to make further, more drastic and more effective restrictions than ever before. While the World War delayed the necessity for such legislation, yet it was soon evident that it had also created a greater necessity than ever before for restrictions more drastic than any previously dreamed of.[114]

This new wave of immigrants feared by Garis and other nativists had begun to come to America in the early 1880s, largely from southern and eastern Europe. This heavy flow of human cargo included people from Russia, Russian Poland, the Austrio-Hungarian Empire, Greece, the Near East, the Balkans, Italy and Portugal. The persecution of the Jews in Russia (called pogroms) caused large numbers of them to leave that country.

This latest migration grew in volume until the outbreak of the First World War; then, it rose up again after the war until the first quota act in 1921 placed a damper on it. Historians have called this wave of immigration to the United States between 1882 and the 1920s the "New Immigration." The Fabre Line was both its promoter and its beneficiary.[115]

American history provides many illustrations of nativistic resentment toward newer immigrants by those who came earlier and were more firmly established. However, resentment directed toward the immigrants coming from eastern and southern Europe after 1890 seemed to reach a more fervent pitch than anything that had occurred earlier, save for the reaction by the Know-Nothing Party to the immigration of Irish Catholics in the 1850s. During the years immediately prior to and through the First World War, many "old stock" Americans firmly believed that these immigrants could not be culturally assimilated or absorbed by America as quickly and completely as those of the "Old Immigration" had been.

After the armistice of November 1918, native-born Americans became alarmed by the demands of recent immigrants and Irish Americans for U.S. support of causes in their former homelands. In particular, Italian Americans urged the Italian annexation of Fiume on the Adriatic Sea; Irish Americans continued to demand that Ireland be separated from Great

Britain; Zionist Jews advocated the establishment of an independent Jewish state in Palestine; Polish Americans lobbied for an end to the partition of Poland; and Ukrainian Americans sought independence from Russia for their homeland.[116] Wondering whether American interests really came first with their newer countrymen, native-born Americans concluded that recent waves of immigration had been too rapid and too numerous for the country to absorb and that restrictions were the only logical means of protecting and maintaining the cultural, ethnic and religious fabric of the nation.

Many old-stock Americans believed that the more desirable immigration from northern and western Europe would not be revived in the near future and that the number coming from southern and eastern Europe would increase markedly. Although the 1917 Literacy Test Act was ostensibly based on the principle of selection, its true intent was to restrict the number of immigrants. When this law failed to stem the tide of immigration, Congress instituted the quota system.

The Emergency Quota Act of 1921 limited immigration from any one country to 3 percent of the number of foreign-born people of that nationality residing in the United States according to the census of 1910. The maximum limit on the total number of immigrants admitted into the country during any one year was placed at 357,803.

Three years later, Congress passed a more restrictive measure, the Reed-Johnson Act of 1924, or the National Origins Quota Act. Signed by President Calvin Coolidge two days after its passage, it reduced the 1921 quota of 3 percent to 2 percent, changed the base year from 1910 to 1890 (a date when the "new" immigration had just begun) and halved the maximum limit on total annual immigration to 164,667. Both acts were aimed at the immigration from southern and eastern Europe, and according to the language of the 1924 law, they effectively accomplished their intended purpose: to maintain the "racial preponderance [of] the basic strain of our people, and thereby to stabilize the ethnic composition of the population."

Statistics show that immigration from Mediterranean countries was reduced in subsequent years to a mere trickle. By changing the base year of 1910 to 1890, the 1924 law drastically reduced the number of "new" immigrants that were allowed admission by the 1921 act, because far fewer people from countries in southern and eastern Europe were residing in the United States in 1890 than in 1910. The 1924 law carried a provision to be implemented in 1927, at which time the base year would change to 1920, but the total number of immigrants admitted per year would be cut

IMMIGRATION TO RHODE ISLAND

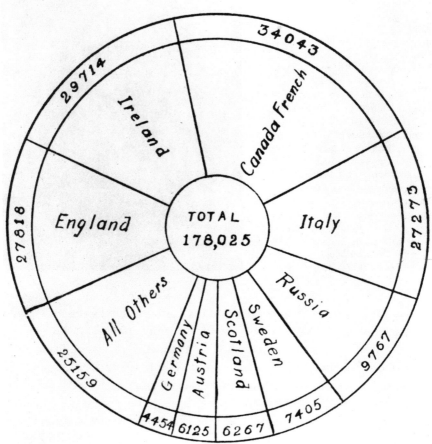

DIAGRAM BY JOHN J. SCOLNICK

Demographer John J. Scolnick prepared this pie chart of Rhode Island's foreign-born population based on the 1910 federal census. Notable are the number of Italian-born residents (27,273) and the fact that the Portuguese were not given the separate slice merited by their foreign-born tally of 6,068. A similar pie chart, based on the 1890 census, would list only 2,468 Italian-born residents, thus furnishing a graphic example of the most discriminatory feature of the 1924 quota law. In this chart, the segments allotted to Russia and Austria represent significant numbers of Polish Catholics and immigrants of the Jewish faith (Poland was then partitioned). Significant Irish immigration, which began in the 1820s, produced a large number of foreign-born residents from Ireland. Long overlooked but quite substantial in Rhode Island was the English migration to industrial America that occurred in the late nineteenth century. All English immigrants did not come on the *Mayflower*. *Conley Collection.*

LeBaron Bradford Colt (1846–1924), as his three names indicate, was descended from several prominent Bristol families. After twenty-nine years of competent service as the presiding judge of the U.S. Court of Appeals for the First Circuit, Colt was elected as a Republican to the U.S. Senate in 1913, becoming the last Rhode Island senator to be chosen by the general assembly. He acquired the chairmanship of the Senate Committee on Immigration on March 4, 1919, and served in that capacity until his death at Linden Place in Bristol on August 18, 1924. Colt unsuccessfully resisted the discriminatory aspects of the 1924 Immigration and Nationality Act, particularly its use of the 1890 federal census as the standard for the quota system and that statute's provision defining the Japanese as aliens ineligible for citizenship. *Photo courtesy of the Rhode Island Heritage Hall of Fame.*

to 150,000. Owing to strong opposition from American religious and ethnic groups whose people were targeted by the act, from employers who feared a shortage of labor and from those who favored the free migration of peoples, this reduced annual quota was delayed until July 1, 1929.[117]

Rhode Islander LeBaron Bradford Colt, a former high-ranking federal judge, chaired the Senate Committee on Immigration when it considered the Quota Acts of 1921 and 1924. On the latter measure, he voted to retain the 1910 census as the quota basis for foreign-born nationals and to reject the patently discriminatory standard of using the 1890 census. He also voted against the motion to lower the annual quota to 2 percent. Despite Colt's position as chairman, he lost this battle with the nativistic restrictionists as well as an effort to prevent the law from excluding Japanese as "persons ineligible to citizenship." On August 18, 1924, less than three months after the passage of the Reed-Johnson Act, Senator Colt died unexpectedly and dejectedly at Linden Place, his Bristol home. By 1929, when the 1920 census became the quota standard, the momentum of migration had been halted, and a worldwide economic depression loomed on the horizon.[118]

Like other transatlantic carriers from the Mediterranean, the Fabre Line felt the pinch caused by these acts. Shortly after the Literacy Test Act of

1917 became law, the line announced that it might be forced to omit calls at Providence. According to the company's records, fewer than 40 percent of its passengers demonstrated an ability to read. The line felt that its Providence-bound passenger traffic might be reduced from an average of about six hundred per sailing to two hundred—hardly a sufficient number to warrant continued calls at the port, especially since there was little cargo handled there.[119]

In fact, the Literacy Test failed to reduce immigration from southern and eastern Europe significantly. Fabre sailings were suspended for fifteen months because of the menace of German U-boats, but the years from 1920 to 1924 witnessed the greatest boom period that the line ever experienced at Providence.

Speculation about the Fabre Line's future at the port of Providence again circulated as Congress passed the Emergency Quota Act of 1921, which President Warren Harding quickly signed into law. To that date, the greatest number of immigrants coming to Providence via the Fabre Line had been Portuguese. The new law placed severe limitations on the number of both Portuguese and Italian immigrants, the groups that had been the mainstay of the Fabre Line at New York as well as at Providence.[120]

On May 14, 1921, D.H.G. Jones of Elwell & Company declared that it was too early to speculate about the future of the Fabre company at the port of Providence. However, Jones announced that there would definitely be no curtailment of the Fabre sailings at New York, where the company carried on most of its cargo business.[121]

The following week, the Providence Chamber of Commerce received a letter from the president of the Fabre Line assuring the city that service would continue "even though the freight to and from [Providence] is practically nil." The president explained, however, that local merchants and shippers had apparently not taken advantage of Fabre's presence. He closed his letter by asking the chamber to help the line develop freight traffic through the port.[122]

In June of that year, a qualification was placed on Fabre's initial assurance of continued service. R.W. Swanson of Elwell & Company announced that Providence would not be abandoned as a port of call, but the number of port visits would be reduced. "We will send ships here at intervals from Europe," said Swanson, "and will have our vessels sail from here when the number of passengers warrants."[123] As the line's New York agents, Elwell & Company was certainly not as concerned with the development of freight traffic via Providence as was Goff & Page, the local agents of the company, or the Fabre management at Marseilles. This can be inferred from statements made by the New York agents that appeared from time to time in the *Providence Journal*.[124]

L. Cyprien Fabre (the son of the founder), the line's president and principal stockholder, came to America during the summer of 1921 and visited Providence in order to gather firsthand information about the possibilities of developing foreign commerce at the port. He also wished to study the effect of the new quota law on his line's commercial pursuits. "Our ships will continue to make Providence a port of call," he told the *Journal*, "provided, of course, passenger traffic warrants such visits. We will not abandon Providence as a port of call for the present at least. Limitation of immigration, however, will make it necessary for us to operate fewer ships into this port."[125] It is apparent that the president of the line had been much influenced by its New York agents. At this time, the line reappointed its local agents at Providence—Frank A. Page of Goff & Page, as freight agent and Mariano Vervena as passenger agent.[126]

A dangerous contest called "racing" came into vogue among steamships carrying transatlantic immigrants as a consequence of the 1921 law. Reports appeared repeatedly in the *Providence Journal* of Fabre vessels attempting to beat the competition to America in order to land their passengers in accordance with the monthly quotas. If a liner arrived in port after another vessel had landed and filled the quota for the month, it would have to carry back all of the immigrants who could not be landed and refund their passage money. This result was costly, and no steamship company could afford to operate under such circumstances.[127] Although the Emergency Quota Act of 1921 adversely affected Fabre's passenger traffic, the company seems to have maintained its usual number of sailings to Providence during 1921 and 1922.[128]

During July 1923, the Fabre Line notified authorities of its desire to renew its lease at the state pier. The lease was not due to expire until April 1, 1924, so the line apparently entertained little thought of quitting Providence in the near future.[129]

In an effort to diversify its human cargo along national lines and thereby sail with a fuller complement of eligible immigrants, the Fabre Line began to move eastward in the Mediterranean by 1923. During the first half of that year, the immigrants from southeastern Europe and the Near East were transported by smaller steamships westward within the Mediterranean to Fabre's big transatlantic liners and then carried by the Fabre steamers to America. At this time, the *Providence Journal* began to inform its readers of the number of each nationality disembarking at Providence. These immigrants included persecuted Armenians from Turkey, Christian Syrians and Lebanese escaping from Muslim rule, Greeks, Jews from various countries and Ukrainians and Romanians from the Black Sea area.[130]

Landing immigrants under the existing quota law was not the only problem that the Fabre Line encountered during the early 1920s. Occasionally, its capital equipment suffered breakdowns. The *Roma*, an old veteran of the line, incurred a mechanical failure in Providence Harbor upon its arrival on October 11, 1923. It had sustained a broken main shaft on its passage from New York and was unable to continue its intended Atlantic sailing. Its two hundred passengers were transferred to the *Canada*, which arrived the next day destined for Naples, and the *Roma* then returned to New York for repairs.[131]

By the early months of 1924, an eastern route had become a new sailing pattern for the Fabre Line. Vessels left Marseilles and sailed to Alexandria, Egypt; then to Lebanon, Syria, and Turkish ports; and then into the Black Sea to Constanza, Romania, which was about two hundred miles south of the Ukrainian seaport of Odessa. The return included calls at Greek and Italian ports, with ships sometimes making a call at Algiers before clearing the Mediterranean for Lisbon and the Azores and on to Providence and New York. Fabre vessels did not call regularly at all of the eastern Mediterranean ports named here, but during a two-month period, they usually managed to visit each of them. In some of these countries, the line varied its ports of call. All of the sailings at this time included calls at the Azores, and most included Lisbon. Fabre steamers still continued to ply the older route from Marseilles, Naples, Lisbon and the Azores to America, but the new and more diverse cruising pattern continued during the remainder of the line's days at Providence.

The new route into the eastern Mediterranean took from thirty to thirty-five days, compared with the twelve- to fifteen-day passage time of the old route, and it consumed 6,500 nautical miles. At first, only the smaller vessels of the line plied the eastern route, but by the late 1920s, the larger *Canada*, *Patria* and *Providence* were also sailing to the eastern Mediterranean.[132]

Because of the delay and congestion at the port of New York occasioned by the increased inspection that the 1921 law required, the Fabre Line considered disembarking all of its passengers at Providence. Various government agencies whose personnel met the Fabre vessels believed that they would be able to process the line's immigrant passengers much more quickly there. This policy was implemented in 1924.[133] By that summer, Fabre was disembarking immigrants bound for New York at Providence. These

The influx of immigrants to Rhode Island—many brought by the Fabre Line—aroused nativist resentment through the early decades of the twentieth century. In the postwar years, that hostility found expression through the agency of the Ku Klux Klan. The first Klan had been a purely southern, antiblack phenomenon of the Reconstruction era. The second Klan, dating from 1915, was not only antiblack but also hostile to foreigners, Catholics and Jews, and it was national in scope. Klan activity occurred in Rhode Island during 1923, peaked in the following year and then gradually died away in the early '30s. In Rhode Island, the Klan was mainly a rural phenomenon demonstrating the resentment and antagonism that agrarian, Republican, Protestant, old-stock Rhode Islanders felt toward the increasingly numerous urban ethnics. Cross burnings and camp meetings—such as the 1927 Georgiaville gathering shown here—occurred in many small outlying towns. But Providence did not escape the contagion; Klan rallies were held in Washington Park, and in January 1925, one thousand people attended a public dinner-dance held by the Providence County Klanton at Rhodes-on-the-Pawtuxet. *Photo courtesy of the* Providence Journal.

passengers were then sent on to New York via the New Haven Railroad or, sometimes, by Long Island Sound steamers.[134]

The Fabre Line had a good year at Providence in 1924, when the line transported 11,636 passengers to the port and carried away 2,035. Fabre had found that by diversifying the origins of its passengers, it was able to land a greater number in America. The increase was only temporary, however, for the line was soon confronted with the even more severe quota law of 1924.[135]

Immigration to Rhode Island

The 1920s brought some changes in the character of the immigrant passengers coming to America via the Fabre Line. Their average age seems to have increased during the 1920s from what it had been in the preceding decade. There were fewer "birds of passage" (those who came and returned to their native land) and "pathfinders" (those who were bent on earning sufficient money in America to pay for the passage of relatives and friends). Also, fewer were coming as a consequence of economic opportunity alone; many more now came because others of their nationality were already settled here. However, many eastern immigrants who would certainly have come to America if they could have entered the country were settling in France. During the 1920s, it was France, not the United States, that became the major recipient of these immigrants.[136]

Occasionally, reports appeared in the *Providence Journal* of Fabre vessels encountering severe storms in the Atlantic or the Mediterranean and arriving in port low in coal and provisions. One of these dangerous crossings is of particular interest. On March 13, 1924, the New York–bound *Patria*, four days behind schedule because of rough weather, encountered another storm off Nantucket and diverted its course from New York to Narragansett Bay. It finally found itself in Newport Harbor. Captain Pierre Deschelles told the *Journal* of this encounter with the storm, his worst in forty-six years at sea:

> *When off Nantucket light vessel last Tuesday morning, the glass* [barometer] *began to fall sharply, and radio reports brought me nothing but storm warnings from everywhere. I decided, accordingly, that with my supply of coal depleted as it was, it would be unsafe to risk attempting New York. I figured I might be blown out to sea, powerless to cope with the storm.*
>
> *When I picked up the Brenton Reef Light vessel about 8 Tuesday morning* [March 11, 1924], *the blizzard was raging so that I realized it would be impossible for the pilot boat to reach us. After anchoring there until about 11 o'clock, I piloted the ship itself into anchorage off Rose Island in Newport Harbor. It was so thick that we missed the pilot boat on the way.*

Notwithstanding this harrowing ordeal, the *Patria* arrived at Providence on March 13 and cleared for New York the same day.[137]

With the approach of July 1, 1924, the day when the second quota law was to become effective, speculation concerning the future of the Fabre Line at Providence was rife—its changes would lower the total immigration quota from Mediterranean countries. On May 31, 1924, after learning that the new quota statute had been passed by Congress, Captain Laurent Vidal of the *Madonna* intimated to the *Providence Journal* that unless thousands of tons of American and European goods were shipped through the port of Providence, the Fabre company might transfer its operations to Halifax or simply retreat to New York. On the other hand, he suggested that the French government might subsidize the line for its Providence calls rather than allow it to terminate operations there.[138]

There was also speculation that the Fabre Line might even attempt to transfer all of its operations at New York to Providence. The reasoning behind this rumor was that Ellis Island was so congested that the steamship company would find it less expensive to maintain connections at Providence than at New York. Although the landing facilities at the New York port were superior, it was believed that foreign vessels could unload passengers and cargo more quickly at Providence.[139]

As the effective date of the quota law approached, the Fabre Line officially announced that it intended to remain in Providence, at least for the present. On July 3, 1924, the *Journal* expressed the satisfaction of both the city and the state:

> *It is gratifying to be told officially that the Fabre Line management has no intention of suspending the transatlantic service to and from this port. The rumor had spread that owing to the rigid restrictions imposed by the new immigration law on the influx of newcomers from Southern Europe the line would omit its Providence sailings. At the same time, if we wish to have the service permanently assured, we should do all we can to increase our shipments to Europe. An organized and persistent campaign to this end would produce results satisfactory to all concerned.*[140]

Samuel Priest (aka Cohen), a Lithuanian Jewish immigrant who had become a successful local businessman, was optimistic regarding the prospects for increased cargo handling at the port and acted to accommodate it. He and his wife, Pearl, had acquired a large brick building on Allens Avenue adjacent to State Pier Number 1 in 1917 from the Providence Gas Company, which had built the structure in 1899–1900 as a "purification plant" wherein it extracted hydrogen from coal. At first, the Priests used the building for textile processing, but when the Immigration and Nationality Act of 1924 adversely affected the flow of immigrants arriving at nearby State Pier Number 1 aboard the steamships of the Fabre Line, Sam Priest moved to take advantage of the new conditions. Anticipating that the Fabre

Line would respond to the continuing decline in immigrant passengers by increasing the amount of cargo it transported from Mediterranean countries, in 1925, Priest remodeled the building to serve as a repository for Fabre Line cargo, and he formed the Imperial Warehouse Company. Priest's sudden death in February 1926 altered these plans as dramatically as he had altered the building. For the next decade, the structure housed multiple commercial and industrial tenants before it became vacant in the latter years of the Great Depression. However, even had Priest lived on, that severe economic downturn would have foiled his plans.[141]

In July 1924, the Fabre Line announced that the number of sailings at Providence for the year would be increased from five to ten.[142] The company was attempting to do its part to stimulate the port's operations by offering more sailing opportunities for shippers. Perhaps this change was also due to the recently begun Fabre sailings from Romania to Canada, for more calls at Providence did not require a substantial increase in effort on the part of the line. Vessels carrying immigrants (mostly Jews from the Black Sea area) to Halifax usually called thereafter at Providence and New York.[143]

The Fabre practice of disembarking New York–bound passengers at Providence and transferring them via rail or Long Island Sound steamer to New York—an action always taken on orders from the line's New York agents—was bound to cause trouble sooner or later. Trouble came during October 1924 when the line learned that Rockwell Kent, a noted Vermont author and artist, was planning to sue the company for $5,000 because it landed his son, Rockwell Kent III, at Providence instead of New York, the boy's intended destination. Kent had been waiting in vain for his son at the line's Brooklyn pier. The thirteen-year-old lad had arrived aboard the *Britannia* on September 15, 1924, and after appealing to the Red Cross at Providence, he was given $1 and turned over to Travelers Aid, which sent him to New York on the New Haven Railroad. Young Rockwell spent the night in a New York City dormitory for working boys and, the next day, went to the home of his aunt in Tarrytown, New York.

Kent's attorney claimed that the Fabre Line could disembark a passenger at a port other than that for which that passenger was destined only if the vessel was unable to complete its passage. This assertion, said the lawyer, was made clear by the contract printed on the back of the line's ticket. Since the *Britannia* continued on to New York on the same day that it arrived at Providence, it was obligated to carry its New York–bound passengers to New York. The Fabre Line contended that the rail route from Providence to New York was an optional service provided by the company. If any passenger wished to continue on the journey by steamer, that passenger was certainly free to do so. It seems apparent that the steamship company did not make this policy sufficiently clear to its passengers. On December 10, 1924, the *Patria* was seized at the line's Brooklyn wharf fifteen minutes before its scheduled sailing time because of the pending suit, and the Fabre company was forced to post a $50,000 bond to secure its release.[144]

Reports appeared frequently in the *Providence Journal* of Fabre Line passengers attempting to smuggle goods into the country without paying the required duty. These smugglers were often thwarted by such efficient inspectors as Thomas Farrelly and James O'Neil, longtime employees of the United States Customs Service. Both men tell stories of attempts to smuggle in narcotics as well as expensive rugs, usually from the Middle East. Rug-smuggling immigrants usually claimed that the rugs had been part of their household furnishings for a least one year and were therefore not subject to taxation, even when it was obvious to all that the rugs were new.[145]

One smuggling case is especially interesting. A Portuguese passenger named Joao Rodrigues, who was returning to the United States, attempted to smuggle a large amount of narcotics, liquor and Madeira laces into the country. Customs officials found nine bottles of cocaine and two bottles of laudanum in a gallon can mixed with Portuguese marmalade; a quart bottle of rum was found concealed in a large hollowed-out spool of yarn; and other items were found hidden in the lining of Rodrigues's coat. Further examination of the passenger's trunk at the customhouse revealed a false bottom in which the government agents found a small fortune in beautiful Madeira laces and lingerie as well as several cans of olive oil, with a bottle of liquor hidden inside each can. One of these bottles was believed to contain a mixture of rum and absinthe. Custom officials estimated the value of the drugs seized by Providence officials from $2,500, their legitimate wholesale price in Europe, to $15,000, their bootleg value in the United States. The Madeira lace was to be taxed at 75 percent of its selling price in Portugal; the value of the lace in America was estimated at $5,000.[146]

An examination of the geographic features of Providence Harbor indicates that any large vessel attempting to dock or clear from the south side of the state pier would experience trouble if a strong wind was blowing from the north or northeast. Occasionally, Fabre steamers docked at Providence without the aid of tugboats, with pilots usually determining whether tugboats were necessary.[147] On November 22, 1924, the *Canada*, clearing for a westward passage, took more than an hour to back out and straighten into the channel; a gale wind from the northwest swept the steamer out of its intended course several times. The *Britannia*, arriving from the Mediterranean on the same day, also experienced difficulty when it attempted to dock, so it finally had to employ the services of a large tugboat in order to get into its berth.[148] Many examples of such incidents were reported in the local press.

On the positive side, Fabre's newest steamer, the *Sinaia*, was met with festivities when it arrived at Providence in November 1924. A reception and dinner in its honor were held on board, attended by the captain and his staff, local politicians, customs officials, company agents and representatives of the press. This passage was the *Sinaia*'s maiden trip, but eventually this ship would become Fabre's only visitor to Providence in the line's final years at the port.[149]

From 1920 to 1925, the Fabre Line carried a considerable number of outbound passengers from the port of Providence. Most of these were Portuguese.[150] Out-migration from Providence on Fabre vessels reached its apex during this time. On its eastbound call at the city on July 8, 1925, the *Sinaia* was forced to leave nearly fifty would-be passengers stranded at the state pier, baggage and all, because the Fabre company had sold passenger tickets in various parts of New England for more passengers than it could accommodate. Those left behind were told that they would be taken on board the *Roma* when it arrived from New York on July 16.[151]

By catering to immigrant traffic from Mediterranean countries, the Fabre Line managed to maintain its service to the port of Providence during these difficult years. This traffic was severely hindered by the quota laws of 1921 and 1924, the latter of which was especially restrictive. The figures for immigrants debarking at Providence during 1925 show a sharp drop.[152] The Fabre Line managed to hold on at Providence for the remainder of the decade, but passenger traffic decreased markedly after 1931. Although the company weathered the quota storm, it would founder during the Great Depression of the 1930s.

During its era of peak activity, it is certain that the Fabre Line contributed to the growth of Providence, both economically and demographically. In the federal census of 1910, the city registered a population of 224,326; by the 1925 state census, that total had grown to 267,918, the highest number it would ever reach. The Fabre Line's contribution to that increase was substantial.[153]

CHAPTER 6

STEAMING INTO HISTORY

1926–1934

The Fabre Line experienced a decline of business between 1926 and 1934, and it finally slid into the abyss at the port of Providence during the Great Depression. The harsh Quota Act of 1924 would probably have forced the line to terminate its operations at the port had it not managed to hold on to out-migration traffic totaling over one thousand passengers a year until the early 1930s and had it not moved eastward in the Mediterranean. As the Great Depression became worse, all phases of passenger traffic diminished severely, and there was far too little cargo handling at Providence to offset the decline. Although the line attempted to ride out the storm, by 1934, passenger travel had decreased so much that Fabre could no longer justify further calls at Providence.

The line's end came unannounced and unnoticed, with activity simply coming to a quiet halt. The eastward bound *Sinaia* made its last call at Providence on July 4, 1934. Nothing appeared in the press at that time to indicate that the Fabre company had quit the port. By then, the *Providence Journal*'s initial enthusiasm for Fabre's presence at the port had wavered; its reports of Fabre's arrivals had become mechanical, lacking the color of earlier years. Perhaps the paper realized, after all, that the line's days at Providence were numbered.[154]

Often during the 1920s, the *Journal* reported that certain Fabre liners had arrived from the Mediterranean via the "southern route" in order to avoid storms. This southern route was apparently nothing more than a course one hundred or so miles to the south of the normal sailing pattern.

Aboard the Fabre Line to Providence

Fabre's operations were not, of course, limited to the route between the Mediterranean and America; vessels of the line were also plying between Marseilles and ports along the west coast of Africa.[155]

The *Journal* often included accounts of interesting individuals or animals in its reports of the Fabre arrivals. The following is from a September 1926 story written after the *Braga* docked:

> *The passenger list also included one donkey of pure Italian extraction which was being brought to this country by a wealthy Italian in New York City. According to Purser Muret, it was decided to have a donkey race daily aboard the* Braga *on the voyage west, but unfortunately there was only [one] donkey. Some doubt was expressed as to whether the donkey would be allowed to land at New York as he didn't have the necessary papers.*[156]

The Fabre Line lost its steamer *Braga* shortly thereafter when it went aground in the Aegean Sea on November 16, 1926. The *Braga* had swerved to avoid a sailing vessel and encountered sloping rocks at the island of Lipso. Its passengers remained aboard for four and a half days until the *Roma* arrived from Marseilles and carried the stranded travelers on the remainder of their journey. Fortunately, no lives were lost. Apparently hoping for a time to rescue the *Braga*, Fabre left the officers and part of the crew aboard. Some of the furniture and equipment was eventually salvaged, but the vessel itself was lost. The *Roma* arrived at Providence with 271 passengers who had initially begun their passage on the ill-fated *Braga*.[157]

Large passenger vessels crossing the Atlantic apparently kept in touch with each other to warn of ice, storms and other dangers or simply to maintain collective security by keeping other ships informed of their position in the event of trouble. Evidence exists to show that the Fabre steamers followed this practice. The *Journal* reported that the *Roma*, which arrived at Providence from the Mediterranean on March 30, 1927, had kept in touch with both the *Patria*, scheduled to arrive at Providence the following day, and the *Homeric* of the White Star Line "in order that if any one got into trouble the other could aid."[158] This practice may have been a legacy of the ill-fated *Titanic*.

A number of immigrants attempted to gain entrance to America through the port of Providence with fraudulent papers. In March 1927, almost three years after the effective day of the 1924 quota law, immigration officials became aware that certain parties had found a weakness in the law and exploited it to their advantages. Seventeen immigrants from Greece arriving at Providence aboard the *Asia* on February 27, 1927, had secured entrance to the United States by fraudulent means. Aliens departing for a six-month visit to their homeland were issued return permits containing their picture and the seal of the American Immigration Commission. The seventeen Greeks had obtained the return permits of those aliens who had been issued permits but then decided to remain in their native land. By replacing their photographs and repositing the seal (which was located half on the permits and half on the photos), they had used the false documents to enter the country.

Immigration officials in Washington found the fraud by checking the photographs on the return permits with those on the original applications. They subsequently informed Anna C.M. Tillinghast, the U.S. immigration commissioner for New England, of their findings, and she ordered extremely tight examinations henceforth of those entering the country at the port of Providence. The first Fabre steamers to arrive at Providence after the fraudulent practice had become known were the *Roma* and the *Patria*, which arrived on March 30 and 31, 1927, respectively. On those two days, immigration inspectors detained 113 aliens, 24 from the *Roma* and 89 from the *Patria*. These immigrants were transferred to Boston on April 1 to await confirmation by the authorities in Washington of the authenticity of their return permits.

William H. Husbands—the second assistant secretary of labor and, at the time, a guest at the home of Rhode Island's U.S. Senator Jesse H. Metcalf—said the practice of securing admission to America by the purchase and alteration of these six-month return permits from fellow Europeans was a comparatively new fraud. The seventeen Greeks who disembarked from the *Asia* in February 1927 were the first large group to employ this practice. During the three years prior to this ruse, the government had issued more than 300,000 return permits, and so far as was known, no more than 50 had been misused in this way.

By April 5, 1927, the original 113 detained at Boston had been reduced to 24. The maximum penalty for forging passports at the time was five years of imprisonment and a fine of $10,000. Most of the seventeen Greek imposters, having taken up residence at Boston and its environs, were located by immigration inspectors, and arrests were imminent. However, on April 11, 1927, the *Journal* reported that only eight of the felons had been arrested; the other nine were neither arrested nor found.

It appears that the acquisition and fraudulent use of return permits was prevalent in Portugal, Italy, Greece and Armenian lands, whose immigration quotas were both small and quickly oversubscribed. As a consequence of this affair, inspectors tightened security at other

When the quota system curbed immigrant passengers from Europe, the Fabre Line sought to compensate by developing a tourist trade and produced this elaborate brochure for the winter of 1926. *Conley Collection.*

American ports, especially when vessels carrying immigrants from the Mediterranean were calling.[159]

During the second half of the 1920s, the Fabre Line began to carry a few vacationers, both Europeans visiting America and Americans visiting Europe. Dr. Robert G. Albion, a noted maritime historian, once related that when he inquired about taking passage on a Fabre vessel, he was told by one familiar with the line that it was "not for white men"; the implication was, of course, that the company catered to less affluent immigrants, especially from areas of Europe and the Azores where the inhabitants were of a darker complexion.[160]

In 1925, the line commissioned travel writer Warren Hastings Miller to prepare a tourist booklet to attract more affluent passengers. Miller produced a sixty-two page illustrated travelogue containing descriptions of ten Fabre liners, all of which docked at Providence, and their accommodations for first-class tourist travelers. Together with schedules and cruising times, Miller provided glimpses of an array of Fabre ports of call—Funchal, Madeira; the Azores; Lisbon; Algiers; Alexandria, with connections to Cairo; Piraeus, the port for Athens; Constantinople; Constanza, Romania, the port for Bucharest; Jaffa, the port for Jerusalem; Beirut; and Marseilles. In 1926, Palermo and Syracuse in Sicily were

Apparently unaffected by the Great Depression, four tourists aboard the SS *Providence* posed for this 1931 photo as their ship approached Palermo, Sicily. *Conley Collection.*

Fabre Line booklets were designed to appeal to first-class tourist passengers. A page from one of these publications depicts a first-class suite with a private bath on the *Providence*, as well as the dining room and the ship's social room. There are no surviving photos of the third-class quarters occupied by immigrants. *Conley Collection.*

added to the line's travel itinerary. Such journeys were both fascinating and expensive. With the onset of the Great Depression, the latter of these characteristics would outweigh the former.[161]

With fewer alien passengers crossing the Atlantic in the late 1920s because of the restrictive immigration acts, the Fabre Line transported its own small tourist groups, though these always remained a small part of its total activity. One group, arriving on the *Canada* in August 1927, consisted of thirty people who toured the United States and Canada for twelve days. In 1928, Eugene G. Vernon, a former Fabre purser, was appointed tourist director of the line to coordinate this new venture.[162]

The company's major effort to develop tourist traffic began in June 1927, when it announced its intention to send its larger ships more frequently to Providence. Fabre believed that it might encourage tourism to the Mediterranean countries both among recently naturalized Americans visiting their former homelands and Americans of the second generation. The company said that if the plan proved to be a success, it would purchase other large ships and route them to Providence; if the plan was unsuccessful, it would continue its older policy of sending its smaller and slower vessels—the *Britannia*, *Roma*, *Asia* and *Madonna*—to the port.[163]

At the same time that the company was attempting to secure its portion of the tourist traffic to Europe and the Middle East, it made known its intention to receive a greater quantity of cargo at the port of Providence.[164] Even at this late

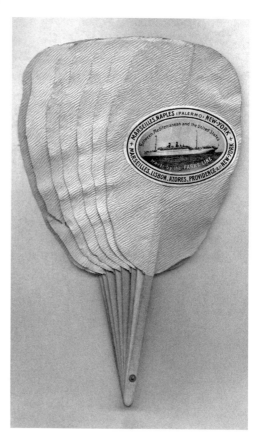

First-class tourists were given Fabre Line fans to ward off the heat during stops on the North African Coast and in the Near East. This souvenir item is a part of the Conley Collection of Fabre Line memorabilia. *Conley Collection.*

date, the company had not given up its longtime desire to make Providence an important cargo-handling port. Although it is unlikely that Fabre still entertained the idea that Providence might replace New York as its major terminal, the company believed that the port could cater to the needs of southern New England more effectively.

Because of the general decline of immigrant passengers, Fabre clearly had to expand in other areas if it was to remain at Providence. This appears to be the underlying reason for the line's efforts toward tourism and further cargo handling. From passenger statistics contained in the *Annual Report of the Commissioner General of Immigration*, as well as the absence of much notice pertaining to tourism in the *Providence Journal*, it is apparent that the line failed to develop its tourism trade to any marked degree. Nevertheless, the bigger and newer ships of the line continued to call at Providence until July 1934. In conjunction with its attempts to increase cargo handling at the port, the Fabre Line opened an office on the second floor of the state pier in June 1928. Theophilus Hamlin was appointed the line's baggage master and freight clerk at the port, with duties that also included the promotion of passenger traffic.[165]

During May 1928, the *Roma*, an old veteran of the Providence run and the only Fabre steamer to call at the port during the dangerous years of World War I, made its final arrival and departure. Later in the year, it was scrapped at the French Mediterranean port of LaSeyne. To replace the *Roma*, the Fabre Line purchased the *Montreal* from the Canadian Pacific Railroad's steamship company and renamed it *Alesia*. The accommodations of the new vessel were much more modern than those of the *Roma*, and it was hailed as a vast improvement for the line.[166]

When the *Sinaia* arrived at Providence in September 1928, the *Journal* reported an interesting cultural development: Turkish women had come from their homeland without being heavily veiled. In that year, the political leader of Turkey, reformer Kemal Pasha (later known as Ataturk), had thrust aside the century-old custom that required native women be so attired. The *Sinaia* carried several young Turkish men and women to America who were said to have been enrolled in postgraduate courses in American universities.[167]

During the spring of 1930, the Fabre Line lost its steamer *Asia*. Recently transferred from the Mediterranean-American run to the Mediterranean-African run, the vessel was destroyed by fire on the Red Sea coast of Saudi Arabia in May 1930 while transporting religious pilgrims to the holy city of Mecca. About a hundred Muslim passengers lost their lives in this disaster.[168] Like the ill-fated *Braga*, the Glasgow-built, Austrian-owned *Asia* had come

PROVIDENCE MAGAZINE

Published Monthly by The Providence Chamber of Commerce

S. S. PROVIDENCE OF THE FABRE LINE IN OUR PORT JULY 8, 1927

THE PORT OF PROVIDENCE, BECAUSE OF ITS STRAIGHT-AWAY CHANNEL TO THE OCEAN, AND GREAT DEPTH OF WATER, AFFORDS UNEXCELLED FACILITIES FOR DEEP-SEA STEAMSHIP SERVICE

JULY 1927

The *Providence Magazine*, the monthly journal of the Board of Trade and the Providence Chamber of Commerce, was a consistent supporter of the Fabre Line's presence in Providence. The illustrated magazine published numerous accounts of Fabre Line activities. *From* Providence Magazine.

into the line's possession via purchase from Brazil, which had seized it during World War I. It was a frequent visitor to the port of Providence during the 1920s, having last called on November 10, 1929.[169]

Oceangoing ships had to be piloted into the port of Providence, so throughout the entire period during which the Fabre Line made calls at

Aboard the Fabre Line to Providence

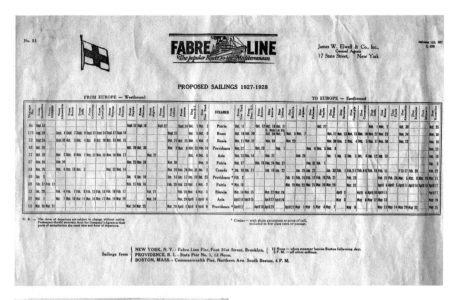

Above: This chart of proposed sailings for the years 1927 and 1928 reveals a wide array of Mediterranean and Black Sea destinations, as well as several eastbound departures from Commonwealth Pier in South Boston. *Conley Collection.*

Left: The *Providence* and the flag of the Fabre Line are featured in this colorful late 1920s brochure listing the ship's ports of call. Here it appears that the *Providence* is leaving the Bay of Naples, with Mount Vesuvius in the background. *Conley Collection.*

the harbor, there was a fierce competition among the state's pilots for this business. The *Journal* spoke of the competition as a "pilot war," and indeed, it seemed to be just that during 1927 and 1928, when accounts of it became more numerous. An attempt to work out a peace among these local navigators was made by means of a "pool," in which each pilot was apportioned his share of the business.

Not all of the pilots went along with this pooling arrangement. During the spring of 1927, two pilots, racing out into the Atlantic to meet vessels headed for Narragansett Bay, were lost somewhere off No Man's Land south of Martha's Vineyard. Despite this tragedy, an attempt to reach an agreement among the pilots failed.

Without question, the principal opponent of the pilots' pool was Tal Dodge of Block Island, the state's best-known and most successful pilot. David Patten, a former managing editor of the *Providence Journal* and *Evening Bulletin*, describes Tal Dodge in his reminiscent *Rhode Island Story* as a pilot "who went up and down the bay flouting all rules and laws [and]...always in a stew with the pilot commissioners and the steamboat inspectors." It may well have been Tal who started the pilots' practice of racing far into the Atlantic to get their ship. In August 1911, the *Journal* reported that when the *Germania* was approaching Narragansett Bay, Tal tricked the other pilots by leaving "his own launch at Block Island, in plain sight of the other pilots and... [hiring] a special launch for the occasion." In those days, Tal seemed to have the field to himself.

Old Tal indeed seemed to be favored by the line, securing most of the Fabre arrivals for himself during the line's early years at Providence. When the *Madonna* arrived in Narragansett Bay on August 1,

The crusty and crafty Tal Dodge, a Block Island mariner, piloted numerous Fabre Line steamships up Narragansett Bay and into Providence Harbor. *Photo from David Patten, Rhode Island Story.*

Aboard the Fabre Line to Providence

1911, Clarence King of Jamestown was apparently the first pilot to sight the vessel and the first to arrive off its side, yet the captain awarded the job to Dodge. Addressing the Providence Town Criers in 1912, D.H.G. Jones singled out the Block Island pilot for recognition: "We have had experience with three pilots, and we have found one who seems better than the others. I see him sitting over there, and I want to have a talk with him later." Colorful accounts of Tal Dodge's exploits appeared often in the *Journal*. The following is from November 15, 1928:

> *While state pilot pool members were jockeying to get the steamer* Providence *of the Fabre Line, apparently unmolested by "Tal" Dodge, veteran Block Island skipper, the old warrior from New Shoreham quietly set his plans to grab off the oil tanker* Lightburn *of the Texas Company.*
>
> *As pilot Clarence King was coming into the mouth of the bay at the helm of the* Providence, *believing that the pool had given "Tal" a licking, the Block Islander already was in port with the* Lightburn, *which brought 70,000 barrels of oil from Port Arthur, Tex…"Only two ships came into the harbor last night and this morning and I got mine," Tal declared yesterday afternoon.*

Journal accounts of Fabre arrivals became less frequent after 1928, and we hear no more of the "pilot war." But in view of the depressed economy, it most likely continued through Fabre's final years at Providence.[170]

From 1923 to 1930, the Fabre Line sent one ship a year to the Cape Verde Islands, just west of the African nation of Senegal, usually during the fall. After calling at St. Vincent (one of the Cape Verde islands), the vessels would continue northeastward to the Portuguese-owned Madeira Island and then to the Mediterranean. The sailings were scheduled almost a year in advance, and usually the older and smaller vessels of the line were sent. These sailings were discontinued after 1930, undoubtedly because of their expense in the midst of the worldwide depression.[171]

During 1930, an effort was made to revive the Southern New England Railroad. This project sought renewal of its charter and to purchase a right of way, a roadbed and bridge foundations. The project was strongly opposed by the New Haven Railroad, which insisted that the port of Providence was more in need of other facilities than of another railroad. The New Haven Company suggested that tidewater terminal facilities in the form of additional piers and a grain elevator and such marketing and purchasing agencies as would be required by the grain traffic were more needed than another railroad. The New Haven contended that its own railroad connections afforded fourteen different routes to all parts of the United States and Canada.[172]

In the immediate aftermath of the Great Crash of October 29, 1929 (Black Tuesday), Providence, as well as the nation itself, experienced a sharp economic decline. One student of the city's past maintains that the economy of Providence was already in "a general and pervasive decline," especially during the allegedly prosperous decade of the 1920s. After a series of violent strikes in the textile industry throughout New England during the first half of the '20s, that industry began to relocate to the South.

New England, the home of President Calvin Coolidge—who was often associated with the prosperity of the '20s—experienced a general downward economic trend during that third decade of the twentieth century, despite prosperity elsewhere. Other areas of the country were more strategically located, closer to the natural resources, fuel and materials essential for manufacturing and to the "burgeoning hinterland of the American West."

By 1930, despite its excellent harbor facilities and superior railroad connections to most parts of New England, Providence had lost its appeal as a destination for immigrants by failing to develop a new industrial base of sufficient strength to create jobs and absorb further immigration. In fact, New England was no longer the land of economic opportunity. The depressed condition of Providence and the general New England region contributed to the decline of Fabre's passenger and cargo business at Providence and ultimately to the line's abandonment of the city.[173]

Tragedy struck the port of Providence in the early morning hours of February 25, 1931, when the most disastrous waterfront blaze in the history of the city began at the state pier. Before it was finally extinguished, the pier and the large storage shed on it had been completely destroyed.

The blaze began a few hours before dawn in the boiler room at the northwest corner of the shed. It spread quickly to the underpilings of the pier. William Gallagher, the night watchman, said that he discovered flames under the shed sometime between 3:30 and 4:00 a.m. and immediately turned in the alarm from the box at the pier. Providence fire officials said that they received the alarm at headquarters at 3:59 a.m. Though firefighters rushed to the scene, the pier collapsed at approximately 8:00 a.m., taking the burning shed into the harbor with it. Local tugboats and the harbormaster's craft, as well as boats owned by the Providence Fire Department, aided in putting out the fire that smoldered into the afternoon hours.

ABOARD THE FABRE LINE TO PROVIDENCE

Although Providence lacked a true fireboat, the boat of its harbormaster was sometimes converted to that use. Pictured here in 1924 are members of Hose 15 demonstrating the manner in which they could mobilize to combat a waterfront blaze. They got their big chance in February 1931, when State Pier Number 1 went up in flames. *Photo courtesy of the Providence Journal.*

Inside the shed at the time of the fire was $250,000 of foodstuffs, alcohol, olive oil and other commodities, the greater portion of which had been landed by the *Patria*. This sister ship of the *Providence* had sailed only twelve hours before the fire broke out. The replacement cost of the pier and shed, which cost $530,000 when they were built in 1913, was estimated at $500,000. The state pier was at the time insured for only $150,000, while the total losses were estimated at $750,000.[174] Had the city of Providence not developed the Municipal Wharf at Field's Point, the Fabre Line would have been forced by sheer lack of facilities to leave the port. In fact, some of the line's surviving posters and schedules indicate that from 1927 onward, an occasional ship stopped at Boston instead of Providence after leaving New York for the eastbound trip to Europe. Commonwealth Pier in South Boston was the location for those dockings. Many passengers boarding there were tourists.[175]

Speculation as to whether the State Pier would be rebuilt ended in May 1931, when the Rhode Island General Assembly made a special appropriation for that purpose. These funds, as well as money received from insurance, were used to rebuild the facility.[176] But the Fabre Line never again used the pier; its new berth served to demonstrate the utility and convenience of the municipal wharf, where docking, parallel to the channel, was much easier and the river wider.

IMMIGRATION TO RHODE ISLAND

State Pier Number 1, visible in the background through the smoke, was completely destroyed by fire on February 25, 1931. The first alarm was pulled at 3:59 a.m. by a police sergeant who spotted smoke and flames billowing from the roof of the building. Firemen arrived to find the southern end of the structure enveloped in a wall of fire. Soon, the heat began to ignite the building's support columns. Pumpers were placed on the tugs *Maurania* and *Gaspee* to assist the harbormaster's boat in trying to prevent the fire from consuming the pier's creosote-covered pilings. A team of firemen from Hose 2 joined the fight by manning a raft, and at the height of the blaze, all five men were thrown into the water almost directly under the pier. Only quick work by the harbormaster's crew saved them. By 8:00 a.m., intense heat began cracking the cement walls and flooring of the pier. Shortly thereafter, Chief Frank Charlesworth ordered all firemen from the southern end of the structure. Less than fifteen minutes later, the entire southern side sank into the harbor with a thunderous crash. Twelve hours after it began, one of the city's most disastrous waterfront fires was under control. The loss of the pier was estimated at nearly $500,000 with an additional $250,000 in produce also destroyed. *Photo courtesy of the* Providence Journal.

Fabre vessels made no calls at Providence during the month after the fire. The first vessel of the line to arrive at the municipal wharf was the *Providence* on April 2, 1931. Sailings had apparently been suspended for about six weeks until facilities at this new site could be made ready for the accommodation of transatlantic vessels. Temporary booths had been hurriedly erected for port officials, railroad employees and others. Steam derricks, loaned for the occasion by the municipal government, unloaded 120 tons of cargo from the *Providence*. All seemed to be satisfied with the initial landing of passengers and cargo at this alternate berth.[177]

The *Providence*'s arrival was greeted with festivities attended by D.H.G. Jones (by then president of Elwell & Company), members of the chamber of commerce and city officials. "Everything worked out well," said *Providence Magazine* in its account of the vessel's arrival. "The first class passengers were at no inconvenience and provisions for the care of the immigrants were as satisfactory as could be expected. Also the facilities for the discharge of freight proved acceptable." This commentator believed that the first use of the new landing place demonstrated conclusively that there need be no fear that Providence would be unable to accommodate the line. Published by the Providence Board of Trade, *Providence Magazine* had always been a strong supporter of the Fabre Line at the port, and on numerous occasions, it had urged the appropriation of large sums for public improvement of the Providence Harbor.[178]

What remained of the old state pier had been razed by early May 1931, and its steel framework and lumber had been sold.[179] By the end of the month, the construction of a new state pier had progressed to the point at which the foundation was ready to be laid. The piles of the old pier had been sawed off at the low-water mark so that cement for a fireproof foundation could be laid over them. The *Journal* reported that the plans for the new structure had been designed to meet the needs of modern shipping and that the second floor, which was to be used for the handling of passengers and baggage arriving on transatlantic vessels, would be arranged to suit the demands of the Fabre company. Unfortunately, the worsening economic climate prevented the facility's use.[180]

During the years when the Fabre Line called at Providence, its only competition came from Cape Verde Island schooners, called "Brava packets." That competition was hardly formidable. Collectively, the schooners brought few immigrants to America through Providence; their main terminus was New Bedford. These small wooden sailing vessels were often condemned because their masters had violated, in the words of Thomas Farrelly, "every section of United States maritime law." Men and women passengers (and even the crew) were not housed in separate quarters; standard dimensions for sleeping accommodations were ignored, as were sanitation regulations; entrance fees were not paid; and people were brought who could not read or write, who had insufficient funds or who were in poor health. As a consequence, the government would seize their vessels and impose fines on the owners, who were often the ships' masters as well. The owners would then generally forfeit

This 1930s photo depicts the two-masted Brava packet *Madalan* docked in Providence Harbor just south of the Point Street Bridge where the Downtown Marina is now located. Here, crew members furl the sails after one of the ship's many Atlantic crossings from Cape Verde—an archipelago of ten small islands with a total surface area of 1,557 square miles located approximately 300 miles west of Cape Vert, Senegal, on the West African Coast. Cape Verdean packet ships visited Providence intermittently for nearly a century, from the late 1860s to 1965. *Conley Collection.*

their vessels to the government for auction. Subsequently, the crew of such a vessel would slap a lien on it when it was sold. Often, the master and the crew were related, and when the vessel was purchased for a small price from the government by one or a number of these relatives, it would sail away with the same master and crew, leaving the government "with the hole in the doughnut," as Farrelly colorfully expressed it.

These Cape Verde Island schooners had no means of refrigeration, no running water and no toilets, and they carried livestock—hens, ducks, sheep, goats and hogs—below decks. The odor emanating from these ships could be terrible. Many Cape Verdeans (called "Bravas" after the principal island in the archipelago) came to pick cranberries on Cape Cod or work in the mills or on the docks. Except for its yearly calls between 1923 and 1930 to deliver supplies, the Fabre Line did not send its steamers to the Cape Verde Islands because of the difficulty its vessels encountered entering the shallow harbor there. Most of the residents of the islands were exceedingly poor and probably could not have even afforded the price of a Fabre steerage passage.[181]

In May 1931, the *Journal* reported that the Fabre Line had merged recently with three other shipping companies, and the name of the founder, Cyprien Fabre, was not at first included in the new company's name. The line was to be formally known as the Compagnie Générale de Navigation à Vapeur. The new firm, capitalized at 15 million francs, controlled more than four hundred passenger and freight vessels. It continued its calls at Providence—where it was still referred to as the Fabre Line—for three more years. When news of the merger reached Providence, some believed that there was a distinct possibility that the new company would increase the number of passenger vessels calling at the port. That hope proved to be nothing more than wishful thinking.[182] Also at this time, the Italian government set up a monopoly on the transport of emigrants, so the Fabre Line sailings from Italy to America were suppressed.

In September 1934, the *Rochambeau*, a large passenger vessel owned by the French Line, made a courtesy call at Providence, presumably to honor

Opposite: The SS *Sinaia*, depicted in this travel poster, was built in Glasgow, Scotland, for the Fabre Line in 1924 and made its first visit to Providence on June 28, 1925. In 1933 and 1934, this 8,567-ton ship was the line's only visitor. After its departure on July 4, 1934, the *Sinaia* became a cargo vessel. In 1942, the boat was seized by Germany for use as a hospital ship, and two years later, the departing Germans scuttled the ship in the harbor of Marseilles. This Portuguese-language poster, and many others like it, were produced by Fabre Line agent Guilherme M. Luiz & Company of New Bedford to stimulate return trips to the Azores, Cape Verde, Madeira and mainland Portugal. A number of such posters are part of the Conley Collection, which contains no comparable Goff & Page posters, assuming some were produced. *Conley Collection.*

FABRE LINE

Ha 40 Anos ao Serviço dos Portugueses—Segurança, Responsabilidade e Conforto

PARA CABO VERDE
[SAN VICENTE]

DIRECTAMENTE NO POPULAR, GRANDE, RAPIDO, E LUXUOSO VAPOR

S. S. SINAIA

9
Dias de viagem com o maximo conforto e Segurança

POR SER UMA COMPANHIA HA MUITO TEMPO ESTABELECIDA E POR CONSEGUINTE DE GRANDE RESPONSABILIDADE AS DATAS DE SAIDA SÃO SEMPRE MANTIDAS COM O MAXIMO ESCRUPULO

A SAIR DE NEW YORK A 21 DE OUTUBRO E PROVIDENCE, R. I. A 22

PREÇOS DAS PASSAGENS

	IDA	IDA E VOLTA	Bilhete de volta comprado Em Cabo Verde
Terceira Classe	$110.00	$235.00	$145.00
Classe Unica (Antiga 1a. Classe)	160.00	330.00	190.00

Sujeitos ao Internaconal Revenue Tax

Na Terceira Classe creanças de menos de 1 ano $5.00—de 1 a 5 anos um quarto de passagem, de 5 a 10 anos meia passagem, de 10 anos para cima passagem inteira. Na Classe Unica, creanças de menos de 1 ano $10.00—de 1 até 10 anos meia passagem—de 10 anos para cima passagem inteira.

A proxima sahida do vapor "Sinaia" de Nova York a 21 de Outubro e de Providence a 22 para S. Vicente, Cabo Verde, deve-lhes merecer toda a atenção, não só por ser um paquete rapido mas tambem por possuir o que ha de melhor em acomodações de terceira classe onde todos os passageiros são acomodados em confortaveis e espaçosos quartos particulares de 2, 4 e 6 pessoas. Nestes quartos os passageiros encontrarão lavatorios com agua quente e fria, bons lençoes e cobertores nas camas, o chão devidamente atapetado e illuminação a electricidade.
A bordo deste elegante e confortavel paquete as refeições são abundantes e frequentes, apetitosamente preparadas por cosinheiros portugueses e servidas numa ampla e higienica sala de jantar.

N. B.—Este Ano Todos os Passageiros são Acomodados em bons Camarotes de 2, 4 e 6 Pessoas

REGRESSO DE CABO VERDE

Como nos anos anteriores a Fabre Line mandará a Cabo Verde na primavera do ano proximo, em data que será oportunamente anunciada, um vapor que trará para Providence os passageiros que seguem no SINAIA e que desejam regressar naquela epoca a America.

Para mais informações dirijam-se ao agente local

Guilherme M. Luiz & Co. Inc.
101 Rivet St.
New Bedford, Mass.

The SS *Rochambeau*, a 12,670-gross ton ship with a length of 559.4 feet, belonged to Compagnie Générale Transatlantique (the French Line). Slightly larger than the *Providence* and the *Patria*, it was chartered by the depleted Fabre Line for a September 1932 visit to Providence, where it accommodated the Fabre company by picking up seventy-two pre-booked passengers at Providence for transport to Lisbon. The presence of the *Rochambeau* in Providence was fitting. Its namesake, French general Comte de Rochambeau, had set off from the Providence waterfront in June 1781 on his army's fateful march to Yorktown during the American War for Independence. Cooperation among the various French transatlantic lines was common, as evidenced by the long-term leasing of the *Providence* and the *Patria* to Messageries Maritimes in 1932. *Conley Collection.*

Fabre's commitment to seventy-two Portuguese travelers who had booked European passage long in advance. Elwell & Company, the Fabre Line's New York agents, sent personnel to Providence to assist with the docking, boarding and clearing of the aptly named *Rochambeau*. Shortly after this ship's arrival in France via Lisbon, it was scrapped at Dunkirk.[183]

Although the *Journal* gave its readers no information that would indicate that this was the line's finale, Providence had seen the last of the big transatlantic steamers whose regular calls had made it a major immigrant-receiving port. Nothing more was heard of the Fabre Line at the port of Providence from this time onward.

On June 26, 1934, the *Sinaia* became the last Fabre vessel to arrive from the Mediterranean at the port of Providence, where it discharged 84 of its 152 passengers along with 152 tons of freight that included two thousand cases of wine.[184] On its eastbound passage, the *Sinaia* made the line's final call at the port on July 4, 1934, and carried away 450 passengers, 150 of whom were from the Providence to New Bedford metropolitan area. Most of these passengers were embarking on brief vacation trips to European countries and the Middle East, though some were leaving for prolonged stays in the Azores or Portugal.[185]

In November 1934, the *Journal* reported that the U.S. Supreme Court had rejected the Fabre Line's appeal of the $2,397 fine that had been imposed on it for bringing two aliens suffering from trachoma, a contagious eye disease, to America (probably to New York) in 1930. Still, there was no indication in that news article that the line was gone from Providence. It simply faded away.[186]

The reorganized Fabre Line struggled through the Depression at New York. The small amount of tourist traffic that the line had developed during the 1920s was usually accommodated there, and Providence-bound cargo was imported at New York and sent to Rhode Island by rail, bonded truck or Long Island Sound steamers (the Colonial Line and the New Haven Railroad–owned Providence Line were then operating steamer service between New York and Providence).[187]

After 1934, the Glasgow-built *Sinaia* was converted to a short-run cargo carrier. During World War II, it was seized by the Germans for use as a hospital ship. The Germans scuttled the vessel in August 1944 when they evacuated Marseilles. Two years later, it was raised by the French and scrapped.[188]

In 1932, the *Providence* and the *Patria*, longtime capital ships of the Fabre Line, were chartered to the Messageries Maritimes Company, which bought

Aboard the Fabre Line to Providence

Like the *Asia*, the SS *Patria* was an ill-fated vessel. This 11,885-ton sister ship of the *Providence* was built for the Fabre Line in 1913 at the French Mediterranean port of LaSeyne. It called at Providence from September 1923 until May 1931, a year before both the *Patria* and the *Providence* were chartered to the Messageries Maritimes Company. In November 1940, after the outbreak of World War II, it was sunk in Haifa Harbor by Muslim saboteurs who planted explosives on the ship. At the time of the attack, almost 1,800 Jewish refugees from Europe had embarked, along with a crew of 130 and numerous British guards. The explosions injured 172 persons and killed nearly 300 others. Most of the victims were Jewish refugees, but about 50 were crew members or British troops. *Conley Collection.*

them outright in 1940. The venerable *Providence*, after many years of service in the eastern Mediterranean, was retired in 1951 and scrapped later that year at the Italian naval port of LaSpazia.[189]

A much more tragic fate befell the SS *Patria*. Constructed in 1913 as the older but slightly smaller sister ship of the *Providence*, the *Patria* was initially a transatlantic liner, the first such ship to be equipped with a cinema for its first-class passengers. After World War I, it became an immigrant ship and made its first of twenty-two visits to Providence on July 29, 1923, and its final call on May 12, 1931. Shortly thereafter, the *Patria* was leased by Fabre to Services Contractuels des Messageries Maritimes, which ran it between the south of France and the Middle East until the outbreak of World War II.

When France surrendered to Germany in June 1940 and Italy declared war on France and the United Kingdom, British authorities in Palestine took control of the vessel in the port of Haifa and placed it under the management of the British-India Steam Navigation Company for use as a troop ship. An intervening event changed its purpose.

In November 1940, the Royal Navy intercepted three chartered steamships—the *Pacific*, the *Milos* and the *Atlantic*—that were carrying Jewish refugees from German-occupied Europe to Palestine. Because these refugees lacked permits to enter this British mandate (i.e., an area placed under British administration by the League of Nations), the English ordered their transfer aboard the *Patria* to British Mauritius, a small island in the Indian Ocean about 450 miles east of Madagascar. While the *Patria* was in the process of loading, Muslim saboteurs planted a bomb aboard the ship. Its explosion on November 25, 1940, sunk the vessel in sixteen minutes, killing between 260 and 300 persons, mostly refugees, and injuring 172. The *Patria* remained a partially submerged wreck in the Haifa harbor until 1952, when it was scrapped.[190]

With difficulty, the line weathered the Great Depression at New York, emerging principally as a freight-carrying company. The name of the firm was changed again on February 1, 1941, to Compagnie de Navigation Cyprien Fabre & Cie, with the word "steam" (*à vapeur*) dropped—reflecting changes in the mode of oceangoing propulsion—and Cyprien Fabre's name reinserted. After World War II, the company's activities were largely confined to cargo hauling. During the 1950s, the line maintained three distinct runs: New York–Mediterranean, Mexican Gulf–Mediterranean and Great Lakes–Mediterranean (via the St. Lawrence Seaway). By 1957, it had become strictly a freight-carrying company. Its last two cargo ships were sold in 1979, ending ninety-eight years of oceanic commerce.[191]

The last recorded Fabre-owned vessel to enter Providence Harbor was the freighter *Bernhard Ingelsson*, which arrived on December 10, 1958. At that time, it was under charter to a Swedish company, which had changed its name to correspond with the nationality of the new operators.[192] The only connection between the ship and the company that had for so many years graced the port of Providence was the vessel's ownership. The Fabre Line, as Rhode Islanders knew it, had long since departed from Providence and steamed into history.

CHAPTER 7

PASSENGERS AND THEIR PLACES OF SETTLEMENT

Passenger service was the mainstay of the Fabre Line at the port of Providence between 1911 and 1934. Immigrant traffic was especially prominent there, with nearly eighty-four thousand aliens admitted during that twenty-three-year span, of which about eleven thousand, or nearly one in eight, elected to settle in Rhode Island after landing in Providence aboard a steamship of the Fabre Line. This figure is around half the number of residents in Rhode Island in 1736, a century after its founding.

Because the line's cargo handling never developed significantly at the port, Fabre's *raison d'etre* remained passenger transport. When that dried up during the Great Depression, Fabre said farewell to Providence and transferred all its American activity to the port of New York.

Before the advent of the line in 1911, immigrant traffic at the Providence port was a mere trickle, but immediately upon the inception of Fabre service at Providence, large numbers of immigrants, principally from Italy and Portugal, came to the city. The transport business grew rapidly until World War I, but sailings and passenger traffic were precarious and sparse during the conflict. The year 1919 was the line's worst because most of its passenger vessels, commandeered during the war by the French government, had yet to be released. The operations of the line sprang back quickly after that, however, and the company experienced its best year during fiscal 1921, when 13,889 passengers arrived at Providence and 5,249 departed eastward.

During the immediate postwar years before the quota of 1921 went into effect, the company had great expectations, both for itself and for the port

Records of the Immigration and Naturalization Service, 1891–1957, Record Group 85
Providence, Rhode Island

Book Indexes to Providence Passenger Lists, 1911–1934. T792. 15 rolls.

Roll	Dates
1	Dec. 13, 1911–Mar. 21, 1913
2	Apr. 18, 1913–Apr. 25, 1914
3	May 4, 1914–Apr. 2, 1916
4	July 8, 1916–June 17, 1920
5	July 1, 1920–Apr. 29, 1921
6	May 26, 1921–Nov. 28, 1921
7	Jan. 7, 1922–Aug. 1, 1923
8	Sept. 1, 1923–June 29, 1924
9	June 30, 1924–Sept. 12, 1925
10	Oct. 1, 1925–Dec. 18, 1926
11	Dec. 31, 1926–Mar. 13, 1928
12	Apr. 8, 1928–July 7, 1929
13	Aug. 9, 1929–Feb. 20, 1931
14	Apr. 2, 1931–Nov. 25, 1931
15	Jan. 6, 1932–June 26, 1934

Those seeking their ancestors from among the eighty-four thousand immigrant arrivals at Providence aboard the Fabre Line can examine these passenger lists available on microfilm from the National Archives. *Print from National Archives website.*

of Providence. Conditions changed drastically with the enactment of the Emergency Quota Act of 1921, which was aimed at restricting the volume of immigration, especially from southern and eastern Europe. In 1923, attempting to secure legal human cargo, the line moved eastward in the Mediterranean, following a sailing route that continued during the remainder of the line's stay at Providence. Thereafter, Fabre's passenger manifests were more diversified than they had been previously, when Portuguese and Italians dominated the passenger lists. By fiscal 1924, the Fabre Line had adjusted to the 1921 Quota Act and still did a thriving business at Providence, but the more severe and discriminatory National Origins Quota Act of 1924 seriously restricted Fabre's immigrant traffic for the rest of the line's days in Providence. When the worldwide depression struck full force during the early 1930s, the Fabre Line chartered some of its more important passenger vessels—including the *Providence* and the *Patria*—to other companies and terminated its Providence activities.

During Fabre's early years at Providence, most immigrants came to America for economic reasons—for the unbounded opportunities that the country seemed to offer them. Repressive conditions also drove some from their native lands. During the prewar period, almost all of the immigrants who landed at Providence were Italian or Portuguese. Many of the Italians settled in the city's Federal Hill section or in Silver Lake or the North End. Others went to Johnston, North Providence, western Cranston and West Warwick, where they worked either in the mills or on small farms. Coming mostly from southern Italy, these Italians were no strangers to the art of husbandry. The Italians also established smaller communities and national parishes in Pawtucket, Woonsocket, Barrington, Warren, Bristol and Westerly.

The Portuguese settled largely in the vicinity of Fall River and New Bedford, with some smaller communities on Cape Cod, the East Bay area of Rhode Island and Providence's Fox Point. A considerable number of Portuguese immigrants, and some Italians, traveled on from Providence to California, where there were growing colonies of their compatriots.

While many Italians disembarked at Providence during these early years, most got off the boat at New York, as they had done for many years prior to 1911, principally because an alternative Fabre route went from Marseilles to Naples and Palermo and then directly to New York. By the mid-1920s, Italian immigrant traffic to Providence had largely dried up, but Portuguese immigrants kept coming in significant numbers. Most of the immigrants that the line carried after 1924, when it moved eastward into the Mediterranean and Black Sea, settled in New York or the New England region.

Aboard the Fabre Line to Providence

Fabre never gained significant numbers of tourists, and it always remained an immigrant line during its stay at Providence. Fabre agents in eastern and southern Mediterranean countries helped drum up business with cogent arguments for migrating to America. Considering the prevalent travel standards of this era, accommodations aboard the Fabre vessels were generally good but not luxurious.

Tables in the appendix of this study present a general picture of Fabre's passenger business at Providence between 1911 and 1934. Statistics relating to this traffic have been obtained from the *Annual Report of the Commissioner-General of Immigration* for the years considered. Unfortunately, each of the tables relating to passenger traffic ends at 1932, two years before the line quit Providence; after that year, the *Annual Report* appeared only in a condensed version, omitting the numerous statistical tables that were part of the earlier reports. Two of the tables in the present study do not cover all of the years between 1911 and 1932 because, in one case (Table 2), the information did not appear until 1915 and, in the other (Table 3), it terminated after 1920.

A glance at Table 1 in the appendix shows that aggregate passenger traffic at the port of Providence before 1911, the year of Fabre's advent, was extremely small, numbering only forty-eight in 1910. The volume of travelers entering at the capital city began to grow substantially after that year. From information in the *Annual Report* and other sources, it is clear that Providence's passenger traffic from vessels other than those of the Fabre company remained negligible during the whole of the Fabre days at the port. Except for a few that came by way of Cape Verde Island schooners, called "Brava packets," virtually all passengers who entered and departed at Providence did so on Fabre vessels.[193]

Statistics indicate that passenger traffic grew steadily between mid-1911 and mid-1914. The number of passengers transported to America via the Fabre Line through Providence doubled between 1912, the first full year of operation, and 1913, the line's best prewar year. Passenger traffic leveled off during federal fiscal year 1914 to a point slightly below the 1913 high. During the three-year period that includes fiscal years 1912, 1913 and 1914 (ending on June 30 of the following year), the Fabre Line carried over two thousand emigrants annually from Providence. Most of these were destined for Naples or for Portuguese ports, both in the islands and on the mainland.[194]

The numbers for passengers admitted and departed during the years 1915 to 1919 show a considerable decline in transatlantic commerce as a consequence of the war. As Table 4 reveals, the *Roma* was the only Fabre vessel to call at the port between July 1915 and April 1918, after which there were no Fabre calls until the *Britannia* arrived in April 1919.[195]

The *Annual Reports* for 1920 and 1921 indicate that passenger traffic at Providence soared in those years and continued high until July 1921, when the first immigration Quota Act became effective. Fabre's best passenger business year at the port was 1921, with 13,889 arrivals and 5,249 departures. During these postwar years, the number that departed increased substantially.[196]

The totals for those admitted and departed at the port of Providence during the two years immediately after 1921 declined drastically. Surprisingly, 1924 was a very good year for the Fabre Line; its vessels carried 11,636 passengers to the port and took 2,035 away. Statistics for 1925, the first full year of operation under the severe limitations imposed by the National Origins Quota Act, show another steep decline in the total number admitted at Providence.[197]

After November 1923, the Fabre Line began to send some of its vessels to the Middle East in an effort to diversify its passenger manifests along ethnic lines and thereby maintain its immigrant traffic. The line had its agents at work there to stimulate interest in coming to America.[198] Passengers from this area of the world were often transported, via other means than the Fabre vessels, to Marseilles, where they could board ships of the Fabre Line and continue their journey to the United States.[199] However, many of those who went to Marseilles chose to remain in France during this time of restricted immigration to the United States; in fact, France replaced the United States as the leading recipient of these immigrants during the late 1920s because of America's nativistic and discriminatory immigration policy.[200]

The number of passengers departing from Providence declined from over two thousand per year during the early 1920s to just over one thousand during the latter years of that decade. Most of these were aliens returning to their homelands after seasonal employment in the United States, and the bulk of that number were Italians and Portuguese.[201]

The statistics for the total number of United States citizens admitted and departed indicate that many more citizens were admitted than departed at Providence during the 1920s.[202] Apparently, many Americans left from New York via Fabre vessels that did not call at Providence, or they embarked from other ports by other steamship lines and later chose to return by Fabre vessels that did call at Providence. These figures also indicate that travelers were not as choosy about their return passage as they were about their outward voyage. Fabre steamers were not the most luxurious on the ocean, especially during the late 1920s. No doubt, the greater number classified in the *Annual Report* as U.S. citizens were, in fact, naturalized citizens.

Statistics seem to show that during the 1920s there was still a sizable number of nonimmigrant aliens who came to make money and then depart. Since fewer of these aliens returned than came during the decade, it is apparent that many of them changed their plans and decided to stay in America. This phenomenon differs from that of the previous decade, when the figures for nonimmigrants arriving and departing were approximately equal. The mainstay of Fabre's passenger traffic during its days at Providence was aliens, both immigrant and nonimmigrant.[203] When that trade began to dry up during the first half of the 1930s, the line was no longer able to continue at the port.

Table 2 in the appendix to this study lists the future destination of those immigrating to America through the port of Providence. The figures show that prior to the enactment of the first quota law in 1921, the states that received the largest number of these alien arrivals were Massachusetts, Rhode Island and California, with the Bay State leading all others by a wide margin. The majority of immigrants debarking at Providence were Portuguese; the majority of those who remained in Rhode Island were Italian, with the Portuguese following a close second.[204]

A large number of Portuguese immigrants entering America at Providence were bound for California, where Azorean sailors engaged in the nineteenth-century whale fishery had settled. Most, however, went to the Fall River–New Bedford area, the main whaling center, where a heavy concentration of this nationality currently resides. Others took up residence in Fox Point, the Blackstone Valley, the East Bay and Aquidneck Island towns of Rhode Island and on Cape Cod. As with the Italians, Portuguese immigration was stimulated and attracted by communities of Portuguese who had arrived previously.[205]

The statistics after 1921 show a sharp decline in the number of immigrants destined for Massachusetts, Rhode Island and California and an increase in the number of those who were to reside in New York, Pennsylvania, New Jersey, Ohio and Illinois. The number of immigrants bound for Connecticut remained about the same during the entire Fabre period at Providence.

After 1921, the final destinations of immigrants arriving at the port of Providence were not as geographically concentrated as they had been earlier, and by the latter years of Fabre's presence at the port, New York State had become the leading recipient of immigrants who had entered at Providence. With one-third of the total passenger traffic that disembarked at

Providence bound for New York, New Jersey and Pennsylvania, Fabre had no compelling reason to continue calling at Providence, especially since little cargo was being handled there. Fabre passengers arriving at Providence and settling in Rhode Island and Massachusetts were less than one-third of the total number of arrivals at the port during the latter half of the 1920s and early 1930s.

For the period from 1915 to 1932, where figures are available (as reproduced in Table 2), Rhode Island, with 7,661 intended future residents, ranked third behind Massachusetts (22,881) and New York (8,957); California was a surprising fourth, with 5,975 aliens listing the Golden State as their destination. An extrapolation for the productive years 1911 through 1914, when 26,397 entered, would bring the Rhode Island residency total to about 11,000. In addition, there were a great many others over the years, especially Italians, who came directly to New York on Fabre vessels and then traveled on to Rhode Island via other means of transport.[206]

Although the Fabre Line's immigrants scattered to various parts of the country, with a few French arrivals even venturing to Quebec, it is quite evident that the large number who remained in Rhode Island took up residence either in Providence or the Blackstone Valley, where jobs were then plentiful. After Providence, Woonsocket achieved the greatest degree of ethnic diversity from the human cargo of the Fabre Line.[207] Fortunately for historians, genealogists and (especially) the descendants of all these daring and intrepid migrants, lists containing their identities have been preserved by immigration officials and are stored at and available from the National Archives for a very reasonable fee.[208]

Table 3 in the appendix lists the destinations of those departing America by Fabre vessels at the ports of New York and Providence. The information obtained from the *Annual Reports* to construct this chart does not appear after 1920, but the table tells us much about the nature of outgoing passenger traffic via the Fabre Line during the early years of its stay at Providence. The foreign port receiving the most Fabre passengers from both American ports—especially from New York—was Naples. With regard to the total numbers disembarking in the Azores and at Lisbon, Providence outdistanced New York. The figures make it clear that New York received the lion's share of the line's eastbound traffic. At Providence, the Fabre Line was principally a Portuguese line, especially for outbound traffic. New York remained the favorite port of Italians; the Azores belonged to Providence.[209]

The federal Bureau of Immigration kept detailed statistics from 1898 to 1932 on the ethnicity and destination of all aliens arriving in the ports of the United States. During this thirty-four-year span, those Italians coming into all ports and designating Rhode Island as their destination numbered 54,973. Of these, 51,919 were from the south of Italy (mostly rural peasants, disparagingly called *contadini*) and 3,054 from the more urbanized and culturally distinct north. Those Portuguese arrivals in these same years (many of whom came to Providence after 1911 via the Fabre Line) numbered around 20,000. The Fabre Line's local presence accounted for the great number of returnees (some permanent, some temporary) for both Italians and Portuguese. From 1908 to 1932, the period for which return statistics have been compiled, over 13,000 Italians and 7,000 Portuguese were listed as "emigrant aliens departing" from the port of Providence. No other local ethnic groups had anywhere near such high rates of return.[210]

A considerable amount of passenger traffic from New York was destined for Greece and Turkey during the years 1919 and 1920. The line may have been shuttling passengers from Marseilles and Naples to eastern Mediterranean ports, although it does not appear that Fabre's transatlantic steamers were cruising the eastern Mediterranean at this early date. Fabre ships sailing from New York without calling at Providence visited at Italian ports, principally Naples and Palermo, Sicily. Fabre ships calling at Providence did not do so.

The liners out of New York in the immediate postwar were Fabre's larger and newer vessels—the *Patria*, the *Canada* and, after June 1920, the *Providence*. The smaller and older ships used on the Providence run were not calling at eastern Mediterranean ports until the last months of 1923, and the bigger and newer vessels that occasionally called at Providence did not go into the eastern Mediterranean until later in the decade. The *Roma*, *Britannia* and *Madonna* were the pathfinders for the eastern Mediterranean cruisings, with the larger vessels following later. The passage that included calls in the eastern Mediterranean and Black Sea consumed thirty to thirty-five days. Passage time on the old run from Marseilles, Naples, Lisbon and the Azores to Providence and New York was between twelve and fifteen days, depending on conditions in the Atlantic.[211]

Table 4 in the appendix has been constructed from the "Record of Entrances and Clearances of Vessels Engaged in Foreign Trade" for the port of Providence. Fabre sailings varied at Providence for many reasons: the impact of World War I, the immigration quota acts of 1921 and 1924, the practice at various times of disembarking New York–bound passengers at Providence to avoid the congestion at the larger port, the slowing of Italian immigration after the accession to power of Benito Mussolini in 1923 and the general shift in sailing patterns toward the eastern Mediterranean and the Black Sea during the mid-1920s and early '30s, which doubled the time required to complete a passage. These variables contributed to Fabre's irregular sailing schedules throughout the years.

A few generalizations can be made, however, about Fabre sailings. During most of its stay at Providence, the line averaged two eastbound and two westbound sailings per month. Although passenger traffic was light during the winter, the line usually managed to schedule a complete sailing each month. Starting with the *Canada*, the bigger and more commodious vessels began to call at Providence after the war, and the older vessels of the line continued to visit well into the twenties.

The *Roma*, the last of Fabre's older fleet, called at the port until May 1928, the year that it was scrapped at the French Mediterranean port of LaSeyne. The *Roma* was succeeded by the *Montreal*, a ship that the company had obtained from the Canadian Pacific Line and renamed the *Alesia*. It had been built in Hamburg, Germany, in 1906 and was given to England in 1920 as a war reparation.

By 1927, the queens of the Fabre fleet—the *Patria*, the *Providence* and the *Sinaia*—were calling regularly at Providence. Except for one eastbound call by the *Canada* in July 1932, the *Sinaia* was the only passenger vessel to call at the port until its final departure in July 1934. An examination of Table 4 shows the gradual decrease of Fabre service, with sailings becoming infrequent during 1932 and 1933.

The line's gradual demise at Providence was not only registered by less frequent arrivals, it was also evident by the decline in the number of different ships arriving annually at the port. From a high of eight separate vessels in 1924, 1925 and 1928, the toll taken by accidents, scrapping and the leasing of ships to other companies left the *Sinaia* as the only visitor by 1933.[212]

The passenger manifests of Fabre vessels for both New York and Providence show that a greater number of steerage passengers, percentagewise, arrived at Providence than at New York and that more New York–bound passengers than Providence-bound passengers, percentagewise, traveled first and second cabin. Throughout most of the period considered in this study, the Fabre Line's steamers maintained first, second and steerage accommodations. Tourist class was added during the 1920s in emulation of other transatlantic lines. Passenger manifests also indicate that Providence received a greater number of passengers, percentagewise, from eastern Mediterranean ports than did New York during the 1920s and early 1930s, especially on ships calling at Providence and then going on to New York. During Fabre's last two years at Providence, however, it seems that more of these passengers were disembarking at New York than at Providence.[213]

Aboard the Fabre Line to Providence

Until the line began to fade in the public eye in the late 1920s and early '30s, the *Providence Journal* frequently noted the presence of important people among Fabre arrivals. Persons traveling to and from American embassies in various foreign countries often sailed on Fabre vessels, and upon returning—usually home on leave from overseas stations—many debarked at Providence as well as at New York. Occasionally, an ambassador was among the arrivals.[214]

Fabre passengers went through a standard procedure upon arrival at port. Immediately upon entering the harbor, the steamer flew a yellow quarantine flag and awaited the boarding of public health officials. Their inspection lasted between one and a half and three hours, depending on the number of immigrants aboard.[215] The vessel was then brought to the dock, at which time the immigration and customs service went to work. A good description of the procedure that was followed during the early years appeared in the *Providence Journal* in June 1911, shortly after the initial visit of the *Madonna*:

> *The number of formalities which are to be carried out are enough to discourage almost any enterprising immigrant. The first of these will probably be to land their baggage upon the wharf while the passengers are being kept on board to be examined by a force of immigration officers...from Boston.*
>
> *Because there are no conveniences for handling the passengers on the dock* [the old Neptune Line wharf at Fox Point was then being used], *the unwieldy system of asking the passengers questions as they are met in various parts of the ship will be pursued. As one by one they pass the examination, they will be handed cards entitling them to go ashore. There each immigrant will point out his or her baggage and it will be examined in his or her presence and marked. It is expected that this will last* [from dawn] *until 1 o'clock at least.*
>
> *While these busy scenes are enacted on the wharf, the captain will go to the Customs House and make an affidavit that he does not intend to land a cargo and to secure clearance papers for New York.*
>
> *It is expected that there will be 10 or 12 customs officers on hand to mark the baggage. The steerage baggage does not require a declaration and there are very few cabin passengers. The amount of duty collected will probably be enough to buy lunches for the force of men who will have to come from other cities* [one was to come from New Bedford and the others from Boston] *to do their work.*[216]

The operation was carried out more quickly after the completion of the state pier in December 1913, but the procedure remained substantially the same. After undergoing quarantine examination, aliens would then locate their baggage at the pier and proceed through separate interrogations administered by immigration and customs officials. The former examined the papers of the aliens and asked them various questions concerning their political beliefs (especially during the "Red Scare" of the early 1920s), their moral convictions and their physical and financial condition. Following this interrogation, the aliens' baggage was examined by the customs officers. Aliens who passed the three inspections—public health, immigration and customs—were free to proceed to their destinations.

Aliens who did not pass the immigration officials' inspection were detained in a small wood-frame building just southwest of the pier near another smaller structure called the "contagious building." Here, detainees were immediately given yet another examination, and if they failed to pass, they were transported to Boston, often via a canvas-covered truck, for further detention. Unless a successful appeal was made to the Department of Immigration in Washington, D.C., these aliens were later returned to Providence for deportation on the next outgoing steamer. The expenses involved in deportation were charged to the steamship company.[217]

Descriptions of the baggage carried by immigrants were often quite colorful. Many did not have trunks and therefore tied their belongings together with rope or wire; many carried their belongings in wicker baskets. Adult immigrants usually came with one or two pieces of baggage.[218] Accounts of immigrants' belongings appearing in the *Journal* were sometimes peculiar. "There were no less than 25 birds of bright colors and many varieties and sizes, each carried in wooden cages by passengers," read one account.[219] Another told of a stir at the state pier caused by an immigrant who landed with a small wicker basket containing fifty pounds of solid gold coins. This unusual item was given protection by local police and federal officials.[220] Another account appearing in 1911 is more typical of the times:

> *The customary hodge-podge of baggage, including trunks of varied types, some homemade and others bearing similar cumbersome lines, straw cases, leather cases and bundles tied with blankets and quilts of sufficient colors to make a Northern sunset look like a wash-drawing in comparison, were strewn helter skelter over the pier as they were hoisted from the ship's hold and dropped to be claimed by their owners.*[221]

A report in *Providence Magazine* suggests that the scene had become more sophisticated by 1923:

> *Although there are many gay colors, those who expect to see foreign costumes will be disappointed, for the influence of modern America seems to have reached many of these immigrants before they even start for its shores. On the whole they are a very American-appearing crowd. Only the bewildered faces and their motley collection of baggage give them away. Baskets and bags of all sizes, shapes, and colors are in evidence, while some have all their earthly possessions carefully packed up in blankets or shawls.*[222]

First- and second-cabin passengers were examined before those in steerage and allowed to go on their way earlier. This was one of the several privileges enjoyed by those travelers for the higher fare they paid.

After immigrants had successfully passed through the hands of the government inspectors, they often encountered other problems. Many were confused about the distance between Providence and the next place of destination and were shocked to learn that it was much greater than they had imagined. The immigrants' conceptions of American geography were sometimes extremely inaccurate.[223]

Fabre Line vessels were always greeted by various immigrant-aid societies at the state pier. The Sisters of St. Dorothy from Our Lady of the Rosary parish at Fox Point met the steamers to render aid to their fellow Portuguese. They were usually accompanied by priests, such as Fathers Antonio Serpa and Antonio Rebello, successive pastors of Holy Rosary parish; Father M.C. DeBarros of St. Anthony's Church in Pawtucket; and Father Joseph P. Lopes from St. Francis Xavier Church in East Providence.[224]

Local Italians, though less prominent at the state pier than the Portuguese, also did their part to ease the transition to America of their fellow countrymen. In July 1913, Father Leonardo Quaglia, C.S., pastor of St. Bartholomew's Church in the Silver Lake section of Providence, formed a local branch of the St. Raphael Society, an international Catholic immigrant-aid society, with the assistance of Bishop Matthew Harkins and Mariano Vervena, the Italian vice-consul in Providence and a leading promoter of the Fabre Line. Father Quaglia's initiative was in keeping with the primary mission of his religious order, the Pious Society of the Missionaries of St. Charles, called Scalabrinian Fathers after their founder, Giovanni Scalabrini (1839–1905), bishop of Piacenza, Italy, who was nicknamed "Father to the Immigrants." Beginning on August 1, 1913, when the *Venzia* docked at Fox Point, St. Raphael Society members were on hand to welcome the arrivals from Italy.[225]

Matthew J. Harkins, the Roman Catholic bishop of the Diocese of Providence, sometimes called "the Bishop of the Poor," was particularly

This poignant photo captures the determination of an Italian immigrant family awaiting processing at State Pier Number 1 early in the Fabre Line's tenure at the port of Providence. *Photo courtesy of the* Providence Journal.

solicitous of the material and spiritual welfare of the new arrivals. During his episcopacy (1887–1921), he approved numerous ethnic, or national, churches at which the new arrivals could worship in comfort and obtain various forms of education and assistance. At his direction, the benevolent St. Vincent de Paul Society, founder of an infant asylum in Providence, took on the work of meeting Fabre Line steamships with interpreters to render assistance to the new arrivals by exchanging money for them and directing them to their intended destinations. Society agents James T. Norton and John T. Marshall were especially active in this humanitarian endeavor.[226]

Perhaps the best organized of all the religious and ethnic groups that met the steamers was the Hebrew Aid Society, headed by Archibald Silverman with the sustained assistance of Elizabeth Guny. This organization often loaned immigrants money to get to their place of destination or simply to get started. Silverman boasted that the society never lost a dime of the money it lent to immigrants. This group took good care of their co-religionists and set an admirable example for others to follow.[227] It was helpful to this effort that Rhode Island's most vibrant

Bishop Matthew Harkins presided over the Catholic Diocese of Providence (which until 1904 included Fall River, New Bedford and Cape Cod) from 1887 until 1921. Harkins was a champion of social and educational programs for the benefit of his immigrant church. He recruited religious orders of nuns and brothers and authorized the establishment of numerous national parishes, parochial schools and charitable agencies that benefitted Catholic immigrants, a practice continued by his successor Bishop William Hickey (1921–33). Among Fabre Line immigrants, the Portuguese and Italians were overwhelmingly Roman Catholics, whereas Ukrainians and Christian Arabs were either Orthodox or worshiped according to other rites—Ukranian, Maronite or Melkite—that were in communion with Rome and its pope. Nearly all of the Armenians, Greeks and Romanians who migrated to Rhode Island were of the Orthodox faith. *Photo courtesy of the Rhode Island Heritage Hall of Fame.*

IMMIGRATION TO RHODE ISLAND

Elizabeth Guny met every Fabre Line ship carrying Jewish immigrants from 1917 until 1930. The immigrants, most of whom came from Romania, Russia and Palestine, were given clothing if needed, as well as other services to put them in touch with relatives. The Hebrew Aid Society, headed by Archibald Silverman, loaned money for newcomers to travel to their planned destination. *Photo from Geraldine S. Foster, Eleanor F. Horvitz and Judith Weiss Cohen,* Jews of Rhode Island, 1858–1958.

Jewish settlement was only a half mile west of State Pier Number 1. The old "Dogtown" section of South Providence, first settled by the Irish, had recently become the home to many Jewish families and businesses. With the transition of the area around Willard Avenue from Dogtown to "Jew Town," Semitic arrivals from the Near East and the Black Sea areas found a nearby haven from the persecutions and indignities they had suffered in their native lands.[228]

Another group that was on hand to meet the steamers at the state pier was the American Red Cross, which provided such services as caring for women and children whose friends or relatives had failed to meet them at the pier. Red Cross representatives provided cookies and hot and cold drinks at their canteen, and they often transported immigrants to the railroad station to entrust them to the care of Travelers Aid.[229] Many young women traveled alone to America for prearranged marriages, and sometimes their spouses-to-be did not show up at the pier. Numerous instances of such events are recorded in the *Journal*. It was also not uncommon for young children to travel alone to meet relatives in America.

Pioneer female attorney Helen I. Binning provided free legal assistance to arriving immigrants via the Legal Aid Society of Rhode Island. Binning was secretary of that organization in 1920–21 and became its director in 1922. She and Elizabeth Upham Yates were the first Rhode Island women to run for state general office. In 1920, Yates ran for lieutenant governor, and Binning campaigned for secretary of state as endorsed Democratic candidates. Both lost by wide margins in a Republican landslide caused by disillusionment with the foreign policy of the Wilson administration and a general desire for a "return to normalcy." *Photo from E.C. Bowler, ed.*, An Album of the Attorneys of Rhode Island.

On one occasion, the *Journal* published a report of a three-year-old girl traveling alone from Romania.[230]

Representatives of Rhode Island banks were among those who regularly met the steamers at the state pier. The Rhode Island Hospital Trust Bank and the Columbus Bank, an Italian American creation, sent employees there to exchange currency for the immigrants or render financial aid. Mariano Vervena was president of the Columbus Bank during this period in addition to his roles as Italian vice-consul and passenger agent of the Fabre Line.

Telegraph companies also had people at the pier, and the New Haven Railroad was represented by agents who sold the immigrants tickets to their places of destination. These businesses were not taking advantage of the immigrants; the services that they rendered were indeed useful. To make certain of their probity, the Rhode Island Legal Aid Society was often on hand to help.[231]

One of the more important attractions of the port of Providence was the ease of making train connections from there to points west, including California. The port had little of the congestion and impersonal service characteristic of New York. James Sweeney, an agent of the Boston and Albany Railroad, was usually on hand to sell tickets to the newcomers, who could board that railroad at Worcester, forty miles due north via trains of the Providence-Worcester Railroad. This route was both cheaper and more pleasant than that of the New Haven through congested New York.[232]

The cost of a steerage passage from Marseilles and Lisbon to America during the 1920s was between $80 and $90, with first-class fares about triple that amount. The cost from ports in the eastern Mediterranean was about $125. An immigrant's passage money generally originated in America, with relatives or ethnic-aid societies usually forwarding the price of a ticket or the ticket itself to the recipient in Europe.[233]

One of the most illustrious travelers on the Fabre Line was young Humberto Medeiros, who arrived at Providence on April 18, 1931, aboard the *Sinaia*. The fifteen-year-old lad had traveled alone, one of 213 steerage passengers destined for Providence. He embarked at Ponta Delgada in the Azores.[234] Thirty-nine years later, Medeiros became the first non–Irish American leader of the Archdiocese of Boston in nearly a century and a quarter. In 1973, he was elevated to the rank of cardinal.

Journal accounts of Fabre arrivals often included stories of women giving birth aboard vessels. Norton W. Nelson, president of Goff & Page, recalls an incident in which a woman delivered a child as the ship steamed up Narragansett Bay. When the liner reached Providence, she disembarked under her own power, carrying the baby in her arms.[235] The newspapers also reported a number of burials at sea during the years when the line called at Providence.

Those who remember the Fabre vessels firsthand describe their accommodations as adequate for the times. The newer and larger vessels of the line were better equipped. One source maintains that he never saw a hammock aboard any Fabre ship (indicating that sleeping quarters were in bunks) and that steerage accommodations provided for five or six persons to a room. The first- and second-class accommodations, of course, were markedly superior to steerage.[236]

During its years at Providence, the Fabre Line encountered its share of stowaways. They were usually put to work to earn their passage after they were discovered. Among the stories of stowaways is one about Louis Xavier Sousa, a Portuguese American from Providence, who entered a cabin on the *Sinaia* on May 16, 1934, while it was docked at the municipal pier and sailed away with the steamer. He went into the cabin, he later said, for a little "shuteye." Sousa made his presence known to the ship's officers after two days at sea, and for the next six weeks, he worked his passage in the ship's galley. The young man was able to see the Azores and Italy from the ship's portholes or deck. After his messmates had taken up a collection for him, Sousa was allowed to go ashore at Piraeus, Greece. When the *Sinaia* entered Narragansett Bay on its return passage, the young stowaway was placed in the brig. Considering the work that Sousa had done aboard the *Sinaia*, immigration officials released him before the ship departed. The *Sinaia*'s captain found it difficult to believe Sousa's story of falling asleep in a stateroom and waking at sea—he thought that the whole episode had been planned in advance—and as a deterrent to others who might consider attempting a similar escapade, he wanted to make use of Sousa's services a little longer.[237]

Newspaper coverage of Fabre arrivals included accounts of immigrants trying to smuggle goods into the country. (These accounts, of course, are only about instances in which the culprits were caught by the customs authorities.) The items involved included rugs, lace and other valuable, dutiable goods. Immigrants often attempted to smuggle liquor into the country both before and during Prohibition. Sometimes, the bottles were concealed among thick layers of yams, onions, pineapples, bags and boxes. Dealing with the difficulty of unearthing concealed liquor, customs officials poked such layers with a steel rod, and if they heard a "click" sound, they knew they had found something else. During the days before Prohibition, would-be smugglers were forced to pay the duty on the discovered liquor. James O'Neil, a former employee of the U.S. Customs Service, tells a story about a cook from St. Michael's in the Azores who came to this country in 1928, shortly after the presidential election. When confronted with the discovery of his attempted liquor smuggling, the cook responded, "I thought that Al Smith had been elected." Smith favored the repeal of the existing Prohibition laws, and his stand was sometimes construed by some to mean the actual repeal of Prohibition.[238]

Remembering the Fabre Line's years at Providence, a 1958 *Journal* story recalled when Fabre vessels "were oases where it was legal to get a drink during the dark, dry days of Prohibition."[239] From time to time, newspaper accounts told of Fabre steamers that were required to lock up their stores of liquor upon entering port.

During the 1920s, Providence was the third-ranking immigrant-receiving port along the Atlantic Coast. A greater percentage of Fabre's immigrants in relation to total passengers disembarked at Providence than at New York during the twenty-three years in which Providence was a transatlantic port of call. Male immigrants greatly outnumbered female immigrants during this time, especially in the early years, when so many men came to make their fortune in America and then return to their homeland. Other males used their earnings to finance the journey of their relatives and friends.[240]

The numerous ethnic groups that came to America via the Fabre Line came for different reasons at different times. By and large, the most common reason for coming was economic hardship in the old country, an impetus even stronger than the attraction of greater opportunities in America: the "push" was greater than the "pull." Another common reason was religious persecution. Whatever their motives, newly arrived immigrants generally found a job within a short time, and most felt a real sense of belonging.[241]

The majority of Italians coming to America before 1880 came from northern Italy, but after that date, immigration from southern Italy grew proportionally larger. The basic reason for this migration from southern Italy was economic hardship. Coming from a land with a rapidly increasing population, extensive tracts of unproductive soil, obsolete methods of agriculture, meager natural resources (such as coal and iron), excessive subdivision of land, poor means of communication, heavy taxes and a high percentage of illiteracy, Italian immigrants found America an inviting contrast to their former home and a land offering wide opportunity. Many Italians also came to America during the Fabre years at Providence to avoid compulsory military service, a motive shared by other ethnic groups, especially Germans.

In the early years of immigration from southern Italy, between 1880 and 1900, a considerable number of Italian "birds of passage" came to America but soon returned to Italy. After Italian communities sprang up in the Northeast, however, most of the Italian immigrants came here to stay. Unlike those of the earlier Italian immigration, the overwhelming majority of these new immigrants had been farmers, and very few of them traveled westward after arriving here. By the time the Fabre Line came to Providence, a sizable Italian community already existed at Federal Hill, and it exerted a strong appeal for further immigration. Fabre agents did not find it difficult to attract passengers from southern Italy during the opening years of the twentieth century. Italian immigrants found employment in Providence in jewelry, textiles, construction and manufacturing industries. Many became business owners and entrepreneurs. Other Italian immigrants took up residence outside the city, usually on small farms in Providence County.

The official figures of the U.S. Bureau of Immigration as they apply to Italians, especially the 54,973 arrivals who listed Rhode Island as their ultimate destination during the years 1898 through 1932, clearly indicate that those immigrants from Italy who disembarked at Providence via ships

ABOARD THE FABRE LINE TO PROVIDENCE

This July 1921 photo aboard the SS *Canada* at State Pier Number 1 shows a group of Italian women preparing for debarkation and inspection. *Photo courtesy of the* Providence Journal.

of the Fabre Line constitute a distinct minority of the Italian migrants who chose Rhode Island as their permanent home. By May 1911, when the *Madonna* first arrived, the Fabre Line had been making transatlantic crossings between Italy and New York City for nearly three decades, and the Italian-born population of Rhode Island already exceeded 27,000. Clearly, the Fabre Line brought many more of Rhode Island's Italian population to New York than to Providence. These Ellis Island arrivals made their way to Rhode Island via the New Haven Railroad or on a Long Island steamer. As our title indicates, the story of this migration requires further research beyond the scope of this book. However, one can safely conclude that Fabre ships, both before and after 1911, brought many more of Rhode Island's Italian-born population to America via the earlier Marseilles-Naples-Palermo to New York route than by the Marseilles-Naples-Lisbon-Azores crossing, which did not make its first American landfall at Providence until 1911.[242]

The major reason why Portuguese came to America was economic distress and political duress in their native land. Portuguese mainlanders and islanders began to come in large numbers after 1900, driven from their homeland by poverty, overcrowding, food shortages, unemployment, political unrest associated with the establishment of the Portuguese republic and the threat of eight years of military service. The peak years of Portuguese immigration were between 1907 and 1917. Two-thirds of all Portuguese who came to America during this period settled in New England, mostly in the Fall River and New Bedford areas, though a good number of them continued on to California.

The earliest Portuguese to arrive here in significant numbers were islanders engaged in whale fishery. During the eighteenth and nineteenth centuries, whaling captains stopped at the Azores and Cape Verde Islands to gather fresh provisions and additional crew members, and many of these recruited seamen eventually settled in New Bedford, America's foremost whaling port and later a major fishing port. New Bedford thus became the earliest port of entry for Portuguese immigrants.

Many Portuguese newcomers worked in the textile mills of Rhode Island and southeastern Massachusetts. Others fished and farmed on Cape Cod or traveled straight to Gloucester to sign aboard fishing schooners. Those from the Cape Verde Islands (then owned by Portugal) settled in the Fox Point section of Providence. Some of these "Bravas" made passage from the Cape Verde Islands to the Azores and arrived via Fabre steamers during the line's early years. By the 1920s, Fabre Line ships were making frequent stops both at Cape Verde and the Portuguese island of Madeira.

However, most of the racially mixed Cape Verdeans, who were Portuguese nationals, made a much more hazardous and daring transatlantic crossing than that in steerage on steamships of the Fabre Line. They left their impoverished homeland (which gained independence in 1975) via sailing ship. Though their principal destination was New Bedford, three-masted schooners, called "Brava packets," often arrived in Providence with their human cargo. This packet trade was of a much longer duration than that of the Fabre Line, spanning the years from 1860 to 1965. The last of these adventurous vessels were the *Maria Sony*, the *Madalan* and the *Ernestina*, which made its last voyage between Brava and Providence in 1965. This ship is now a tourist attraction in New Bedford's harbor.

Portuguese immigration was adversely affected by the Literacy Test Act of 1917. Many were denied entrance by this law, but large numbers kept coming. Between 1910 and 1920, a total of 89,732 Portuguese came through various ports to America; between 1921 and 1930, a total of 29,994 came. The Fabre Line carried many of these migrants to America, and almost all of Fabre's Portuguese passengers landed at Providence. Portuguese immigrants were clearly the mainstay of the Fabre Line throughout its years at the port.

Aboard the Fabre Line to Providence

The spiritual and cultural center of the local Portuguese community was Our Lady of the Holy Rosary Church in the Fox Point section of Providence. Founded in 1885, "Holy Rosary" is the third-oldest Portuguese parish in the United States and the only one in Rhode Island that predated the coming of the Fabre Line to Providence. The local impact of Fabre on the Portuguese American community can be documented by noting the establishment of five national parishes during the line's tenure in Providence: St. Elizabeth, Bristol (1913); St. Francis Xavier, East Providence (1915); St. Anthony, West Warwick (1925); St. Anthony, Pawtucket (1926); and Jesus Savior, Newport (1926).

During the early years of the line's tenure at Providence, considerable numbers of Portuguese—especially those from the Azores—returned to their homeland after a short stay in the United States. Their reasons for leaving America varied: some had planned to stay only until they had saved sufficient funds to enable them to return home as relatively wealthy men; others became

In 1911, there was only one Portuguese American parish in Rhode Island—Holy Rosary Church in Fox Point, founded in 1885. From 1913 through 1926, five more national parishes were created to minister to the spiritual needs of the newly arriving Portuguese Catholics. The first of these ethnic parishes was St. Elizabeth's in Bristol, which celebrated its first Mass on April 6, 1913, and began the construction of this redbrick church with a seating capacity of six hundred in the following September. Bishop Harkins assigned the Reverend Antonio P. Rebello as the church's first pastor. The edifice was dedicated to St. Elizabeth, queen of Portugal. *Conley Collection.*

Immigration to Rhode Island

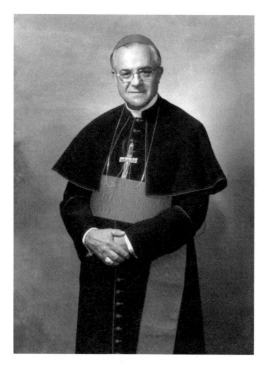

Perhaps the most illustrious of the eighty-four thousand immigrants who debarked at Providence from steamers of the Fabre Line was Humberto Sousa Medeiros, from the Azorean island of St. Michael (São Miguel). He and his family came aboard the *Sinaia* in 1931 and settled in Fall River. Young Humberto, who was fifteen upon arrival, swept floors in a local textile mill for $6.20 a day while studying English in his spare time. He managed to graduate from Durfee High School in 1937 at the age of twenty-one, and he then enrolled at the Catholic University of America in Washington, D.C., where he chose a religious vocation. After he was ordained a priest on June 15, 1946, he continued his studies and earned a doctorate in sacred theology. In 1966, following distinguished service in Fall River, he was consecrated bishop of Brownsville, Texas. Four years later, he was named the archbishop of Boston, and in 1973, he was elevated to the rank of cardinal. During his episcopacy in Boston, which ended with his death on September 17, 1983, at the age of sixty-seven, Cardinal Medeiros was noted as an advocate of the poor and often traveled with migrant workers to celebrate Mass with them during the harvest season. *Photo courtesy of the Archdiocese of Boston.*

disenchanted with life in an industrial environment after remaining in America for a while; and still others sent their families home because it was cheaper for them to live there. Some returned to their native land to marry and then booked passage back to America with their brides. All this travel was beneficial to Fabre's business at the port of Providence.[243]

A few Spaniards came to America via the Fabre Line because of the extreme poverty in their homeland and because occasional stops at Barcelona and Gibraltar facilitated this traffic. With Marseilles the eastern terminus for many of the line's transatlantic crossings, there were also some French arrivals. By 1930, Rhode Island attained its highest total of French-born residents ever when that tally reached 2,013.[244]

A large number of Jews left Russia, Romania and Poland during the 1920s to escape religious persecution by the Communists and other anti-Semitic groups: "To Russian officials [after the Communists had gained control of Russia in 1917] the preservation of old Jewish culture and religion, the use of Yiddish and their clannishness, were roadblocks to Russification." Persecution was the major reason for the exodus of Jews from the Slavic-speaking countries of Europe, as well as Romania; economic opportunity was the most important reason for those Jews leaving Palestine and coming to America.[245]

Some ethnic Romanians, embarking from the Black Sea port of Constanza, came to America during the Fabre years at Providence principally because of economic motives, although unrest and violence in the Balkans drove many of them, as well as some Bulgarians, from their homeland. Certainly the unsettled state of affairs after World War I caused many to migrate, including the six thousand Romanian Jews who sought refuge in Canada aboard ships of the Fabre Line destined for Halifax. The presence of ethnic Romanians in Rhode Island was slight. These arrivals were able to establish only one national parish—St. John the Baptist Romanian Orthodox Church in Woonsocket, the oldest Romainian Orthodox Church on the East Coast.[246]

Ukraine, bordering on the Black Sea with easy access to the Mediterranean, also contributed to the immigrant influx aboard the Fabre Line via nearby Constanza. The twin forces of economic opportunity and anti-Communism sent both Uniate Catholics and Orthodox Ukrainians to America. Those who remained in Rhode Island established three small parishes in the northern part of the state—two in Woonsocket, both dedicated to St. Michael, and St. Stephen's in Cumberland. Another group took up residence in South Providence, only a few hundred yards west of State Pier Number 1, founding St. John's Ukrainian Orthodox Church on Pilgrim Street in 1921.[247]

Immigration to America from Greece occurred largely as a consequence of economic distress; the utter backwardness of the country drove Greeks away. There was then little in the way of religious or political controversy in Greece, but many Greeks left Turkish-held lands to escape military conscription. In Rhode Island, the Greeks established three Orthodox churches: the Annunciation in Providence, the Assumption in Pawtucket and St. Spyridon's in Newport. The first two were founded before the arrival of the Fabre Line, but all were augmented by immigrants brought to Rhode Island on Fabre Line vessels.[248]

Arabic-speaking people, mainly Christians from Syria and Lebanon, also traveled via the Fabre Line to Providence. Economic opportunity and, in some areas, religious persecution were the motivations to migrate. Maronites and Melkites from Lebanon, whose religious rites were affiliated with Roman Catholicism, had established communities and churches in Providence (St. George's Maronite Catholic Church on Federal Hill), Central Falls (St. Basil's Melkite Church) and Woonsocket (St. Elias's Melkite Church). Syrian

Immigration to Rhode Island

Orthodox arrivals joined parishes in Pawtucket (St. Mary's Syrian Orthodox Church) and Central Falls (St. Ephraim's Church). Some of these parishes were founded just prior to the coming of the Fabre Line to Providence, but all of them were enhanced by the arrival of their co-religionists from the Middle East and such Fabre Line ports of call as Beirut and Haifa.[249]

Armenians left their homeland and immigrated to America at this time largely because of religious persecution and a horrific genocide at the hands of the Muslim Turks. With poverty and disease widespread in their native land, these immigrants were also influenced by the economic opportunity that America seemed to offer. Among both the Armenians and Syrians, males began the migration, with most females following afterward. In Rhode Island, the Armenian arrivals stayed mainly in Providence, where they worshiped at St. Sahag and St. Mesrob Church on Smith Hill and the Armenian Euphrates Evangelical Protestant Church in the Armory District. A third parish, St. Vartanantz, was established in 1940 on Broadway.[250]

Whatever the reasons the various nationalities had for immigrating to the United States, the Fabre Line and other transatlantic steamship companies were there to reap the harvest. Passenger traffic was Fabre's lifeblood during its days at Providence, and immigrants made up the largest portion of the passenger manifests. The end of the line's operations at Providence was near at hand when that trade began to dry up (along with American jobs) during the difficult 1930s.[251]

CHAPTER 8

CARGO OF THE FABRE LINE

As noted earlier, often, cargo carried by the Fabre Line amounted to little during its days at the port of Providence. During the initial few years, cargo was not handled at all. The first Fabre shipment of goods to be unloaded at Providence came in July 1914, just before the outbreak of World War I. Imports exceeded exports at Providence throughout the period between 1914 and 1934.[252]

The cargo of Fabre vessels was always classified as "general" by the local customs officials. It consisted mostly of foodstuffs, with an occasional personal consignment of items such as rugs and laces. The company's attempts to develop freight traffic at Providence were never very successful. Although the facilities at the port of Providence were eventually equal to the task, exporters and importers there and throughout various parts of the nation preferred doing business at the port of New York. Businessmen in the Midwest never seemed influenced by the fact that through rates at the port of Providence were as low (if not lower) than those at New York. During its entire stay at Providence, the Fabre Line was sustained by its passenger traffic.

Most local entrepreneurs believed that Providence could not be a fullfledged transatlantic seaport unless it handled cargo as well as passenger traffic. Apparently, there was a matter of prestige involved. Commenting on transatlantic goods destined for Providence and unloaded by Fabre vessels at New York, as well as exports from Providence loaded at New York, the *Providence Journal* decried this situation as early as October 1912:

Aboard the Fabre Line to Providence

Naturally the New Haven road is satisfied with this agreement [that Fabre would not handle cargo at its Fox Point wharf], *for the charge involved in the transportation of a box of macaroni, for instance, from New York to this city by rail, a distance of less than 200 miles, is approximately the same as the charge for ocean transportation of the same box from Naples to New York, a distance of more than 3,000 miles.*

The editorial pointed out that thirty thousand persons of Italian stock resided in the vicinity of Providence, who created a tremendous demand for Italian foodstuffs. Asserting that something more than the prestige of the port of Providence was involved here, the *Journal* maintained that the city was too conservative in promoting Fabre's cargo traffic, and it urged the state to get on with the job of completing the new state pier, which presumably would possess all the facilities (including rail connections) necessary for the handling of freight.[253]

Italian consular agent Mariano Vervena, who was especially instrumental in bringing the Fabre Line to Providence, said that the city would have at least four times as much business going through the local customhouse once the line had fully established freight service at the port. He noted that direct importation at Providence and the lower prices it would bring would expand the local market. Vervena expected that the Fabre steamers would bring goods to Providence from "Portugal, Syria, Armenia, Greece, Turkey, Arabia, Spain, and France" as well as Italy—goods that were then being handled from Fabre ships at New York. He offered wine shipments as an example. Many gallons of wine, which the French bought from the Italians at twenty-one dollars a case and resold to Americans for thirty-six dollars a case, were consumed in Rhode Island and its vicinity. This fact buttressed his claim that direct cargo traffic between Italy and Providence would surely mean lower prices for consumers in the Greater Providence area.

Vervena pointed out that the Italian population in Rhode Island, southeastern Massachusetts and eastern Connecticut numbered seventy-five thousand, with forty-eight thousand of those residing in Rhode Island (a figure considerably higher than that quoted by the *Journal* in October 1912). He estimated that the consumption of Italian foodstuffs by this increasing population then amounted to $4 million. These imports included 400,000 boxes of macaroni (twenty-two pounds each); 75,000 gallons of olive oil; 350,000 pounds of cheese; 15,000 cases of tomato paste and peeled tomatoes; several hundred thousand cans of fish; immense quantities of lemons and oranges; and large shipments of prepared vegetables, nuts, figs, beans, garlic, rice and eggs.

Among the several purveyors of imported Italian products were Frank and A.E. Ventrone, wholesale grocers located at 242–244 Atwells Avenue on Federal Hill, and John Votolato, who operated a hardware store on 1359–1361 Plainfield Street in the Johnston mill village of Thornton, site of St. Rocco's Church. Votolato & Sons proclaimed themselves as "steamship agents" on this 1920s billhead. *Courtesy of Russell DeSimone.*

Most of these imports cited by Vervena came to Providence via the port of New York. He pointed to custom house statistics to substantiate his case: for the year ending September 30, 1913, imports direct from Italy to New York totaled 1,025,960 pounds of macaroni valued at $46,176 and paying duties of $15,289.51; 119,810 pounds of Italian cheese valued at $24,653 and paying a duty of $7,248; and 24,505 gallons of olive oil valued at $32,124 and paying $11,920.44 in duty. All of these had come to Providence in bond from New York.[254]

From the outset, the importation of produce at Providence was stymied. When the *Venezia* became the first Fabre vessel to dock at State Pier Number 1 in December 1913, the enthusiasm of the occasion was dampened by the inability of longshoremen to unload its Providence-bound cargo buried deep in the ship's hold. This unhappy situation was caused by an error in the stowage of the cargo when the vessel was loaded at Marseilles. This gaffe was an omen of things not to come.[255] Providence port workers expected cargo with the next Fabre arrival, but none was forthcoming for six months. Finally, on July 14, 1914, the *Madonna* became the first Fabre vessel to enter Providence Harbor with cargo that could be unloaded. It carried eleven thousand pieces of produce weighing a total of five hundred tons. The *Journal* reported what had been brought:

Aboard the Fabre Line to Providence

> *A smart, lively-working band of 30 stevedores received the merchandise as it was swung over the side of the ship and lowered it to the wharf. There were 10,000 boxes of macaroni, 12 casks of wine, 16 cases of cheese, 630 cases of prepared tomatoes, 24 cases of olive oil and one case of garlic. Among the heaviest importers of merchandise brought by the* Madonna *were H.P. Cornell & Co., 2500 cases of macaroni, 400 cases of prepared vegetables; Narragansett Wholesale Grocery Company, 2000 boxes of macaroni, 10 cases of cheese; and A. E. Ventrone, 1000 boxes of macaroni and 225 cases of prepared tomatoes.*

The paper estimated that the local importers saved $700 on freight charges by having goods unloaded at Providence.[256]

After 1914, the *Journal* did not often describe cargo carried by the Fabre fleet except to insist that the amount handled at the port of Providence was quite insufficient. From mid-1914 through 1918, World War I accounted for this deficiency, but in the postwar years, a renewed effort by the Fabre Line, local merchants and city and state officials to direct a greater share of cargo through the port of Providence achieved little of significance. After the first immigration quota act went into effect in 1921, prospects seemed good that cargo development at the port could be sufficiently increased to offset the curtailment of passenger traffic, and the line made initiatives to develop its tourist traffic as well. Neither effort to rescue Fabre's operations at Providence proved successful, and the fate of those operations was ultimately sealed by the Great Depression.

The timing of the last futile attempt to stimulate the import-export business at Providence was indicative of this failed venture. On October 29, 1929, the Fabre Line announced that the first all-cargo ship of the company to call at Providence would be due at the port in November. This vessel, the *Sevenitas*, was to carry canned tomatoes, tomato paste, olive oil, olives and preserves consigned to merchants in the Providence area. The cargo was typical of that carried by the passenger vessels. The larger shipment seems to have been precipitated by a fear that the existing tariffs on Italian and Portuguese foodstuffs were about to be increased. Importers were stocking up before these tariffs were raised. Ironically, the cargo ship announcement came on "Black Tuesday," the day the New York Stock Market crashed, precipitating the Great Depression. The *Sevenitas* never returned after its first visit.[257]

In addition to the products already mentioned, the goods most commonly carried to the port of Providence by the Fabre Line were liquor, Madeira lace, yams from Portuguese ports, wines, linguisa, meats, sisal grass (used in making rope), Malaga grapes, spaghetti and rugs from the Middle East.[258]

Immigration to Rhode Island

When the Fabre Line began to make calls in the eastern Mediterranean after 1923, passengers who boarded there often brought fine oriental rugs with them, declaring that they had been part of their household for at least one year's time, an assertion intended to make these items exempt from a customs duty. However, it was obvious to custom officials that these rugs would command a high price in America and that they were not part of the normal household furnishings of these newcomers of modest means. Often, officials would challenge the immigrants and demand that they pay the proper duty, but in most cases, the immigrants had their way and the government ended up (to use custom officer Thomas Farrelly's phrase) with "the hole in the doughnut."[259]

A general assessment was sometimes made on the value of cargo consignments in the event of spoilage or some unforeseen accident to the vessel carrying the goods. One such case is illustrative of this practice. When the *Roma* scraped its bottom on the dangerous shoals at No Man's Land off Gay Head (Martha's Vineyard) during February 1917, sustaining damage to its hull plating, a general assessment of 5 percent was levied against the owners of the cargo aboard. The rule by which the assessment was made was one that compelled owners of cargo on board a steamer or any other vessel that met with an accident to pay the vessel's owners a proportionate share for the damage incurred. This same rule provided that the owners of saved cargo pay their share toward any that might have been jettisoned in time of trouble.[260]

The Fabre Line handled much more imported than exported cargo at Providence, despite Rhode Island's position as a major center for the production of textiles, jewelry, silverware, tools, machinery and rubber goods. Reports of U.S. water-borne commerce show almost no cargo exported from Providence to ports visited by the Fabre Line in the Azores and the Mediterranean, save for a small quantity classified as "general" or "provisions." However, a small number of automobiles were exported from Providence over the years.[261]

During the time when Fabre vessels called at Providence, the port carried on a lively trade in lumber, oil and coal with other shipping lines. Providence was then an important lumber distribution center. Its facilities at the municipal wharf were used for unloading and storing lumber cargoes that had been shipped from the Pacific Coast via the Panama Canal. Lumber arriving by this route could compete in price with that brought east by rail from places as far west as Michigan.

Occasionally, consignments of lumber were shipped from the port of Providence via Fabre vessels to the Cape Verde Islands. Wilkes Barre Pier, on

Aboard the Fabre Line to Providence

The Mexican Petroleum Corporation and the Seaconnet Coal Company of C.H. Sprague & Son had docks just a few hundred feet north of State Pier Number 1, and the Harris Lumber Company had large piers (destroyed by the hurricane of 1938) just a few hundred feet south. The importation of oil, coal and lumber by these firms for regional distribution created constant commercial activity surrounding the state facility. The setup at State Pier Number 1 was not conducive to the handling of bulk cargo, so the Fabre Line had to be content with importing foodstuffs, clothing and expensive household furnishings, especially rugs. Shown here is the Seaconnet Coal Company as it appeared in 1905; its related successor, Sprague Energy, still occupies the site. *Photo courtesy of the Rhode Island Historical Society.*

the East Providence side of Providence Harbor, emerged as a coal-receiving center, with coal reshipped by train from there to Greater Boston and Worcester. A fire at the East Providence pier in 1930 brought a temporary halt to this activity, but the facility was later rebuilt, and the coal trade thrived again. By the 1930s, Providence also received large shipments of oil from ports in the Gulf of Mexico. Although these three products were plentiful at Providence, their shipment as bulk cargo via the Fabre Line to the Azores or the Mediterranean area never developed.[262]

Cargo was loaded and unloaded at the state pier with the use of nets. The number of longshoremen needed for handling cargo arriving at the port depended upon the amount and type of the cargo. Three or four men were usually employed in loading or unloading, although the number could vary. In the early years of the line, many of these longshoremen were of Italian stock, but gradually, Portuguese, including Cape Verdeans, came to dominate the harbor's workforce.

Samuel Priest's Imperial Warehouse Company building looked like this in 2006, prior to the completion by Patrick and Gail Conley of its second major renovation and its listing on the National Register of Historic Places as the Conleys' Wharf Building. Priest, whose wife, Pearl, acquired the structure form the Providence Gas Company in 1917, had first remodeled it in 1925 to serve as a warehouse for Fabre Line cargo. This renovation converted the former gas extraction plant from three to four levels. Priest's unexpected death in 1926 aborted that venture, but the anticipated large-scale importation of cargo from the Mediterranean via the Fabre Line never materialized. *Conley Collection.*

Provisions needed on the Fabre vessels were hardly ever obtained at Providence; New York was generally the source. This was true also of the coal used—and all of the Fabre vessels were coal burners. Only in the event of an emergency or on the rare occasion when a vessel originated its outward passage from Providence were supplies of coal obtained locally, despite the abundance of coal available at the harbor.[263]

Measured against the company's total operations, cargo handling remained an ancillary activity throughout the whole of the Fabre Line's operations at Providence. Both the Fabre company and the Providence community made several serious efforts to develop cargo traffic at the port, especially after the enactment of the 1924 quota law. A notable example of this hope was Samuel Priest's retrofitting of the former Providence Gas Company purifier plant adjacent to the state pier in 1925 as the Imperial Warehouse Company, but with Priest's death in 1926, this venture also died.

Aboard the Fabre Line to Providence

The century-old, partially completed twin storage facilities of the Terminal Warehouse Company epitomize the failure of Providence to develop as a port capable of handling international trade. This complex was built in 1913 at the foot of Oxford Street by entrepreneurs anticipating the simultaneous arrival of the Grand Trunk Railroad and the Fabre Line. It is equidistant from State Pier Number 1 and the Harbor Junction dock, located at the end of Thurbers Avenue. Promoters hoped that the Grand Trunk would tap the produce and products of Canada and that the Fabre Line would carry them to Europe and elsewhere. These two huge five-story brick structures were originally intended as end pieces of a far larger complex that was never built. After dreams of abundant cargo evaporated, the structures became warehouses for the Shepard Company, one of Providence's two largest department stores. When Shepard succumbed to shopping mall competition in 1974, Cumberland Farms, a convenience store chain of Rhode Island origin, acquired ownership and held the site in anticipation of the redevelopment of the Allens Avenue waterfront. With the failure of the city to implement its own plan to rezone this area from marine industrial (W-3) to mixed use in 2009, scrapyards sprang up on both sides of the buildings. This second major roadblock to economic viability prompted the owner to demolish them. That process, occurring on the centennial of their construction, is underway as this volume goes to press. This 2007 photo depicts the forlorn state of these warehouses as they awaited yet another promising development that was doomed to failure. *Conley Collection.*

Despite repeated efforts, the existing pattern of routing cargo through the port of New York remained too strong to change. Cargo was a large part of the Fabre business at New York, and had many passengers not shown a preference for disembarking at Providence, the Fabre presence in Narragansett Bay would have been a short one indeed.

FORE AND AFT

A SUMMATION

Acute congestion at the port of New York at the end of the first decade of the twentieth century caused the Fabre Line to choose Providence as a port of call for some of its transatlantic steamers destined for New York. Rhode Island's capital city exhibited renewed maritime vigor, made significant harbor improvements and maintained excellent rail connections with other parts of the nation via the New Haven Railroad. In addition, the future promised direct connection between Providence and Canada by way of the Southern New England, Central Vermont and Canadian Grand Trunk Railroads. Also, large numbers of Italian and Portuguese families, groups that were important patrons of the Fabre Line at New York, resided in southern New England, and they could attract others of their countrymen to the area and purchase imported foodstuffs and other products from their homelands.

Fabre's operations at Providence commenced in May 1911, when the *Madonna* made the line's initial call at the port. The steamship company held high expectations for its operations at Providence, and it got off to a good start that continued until 1914, when World War I erupted and dampened the line's activities both at New York and Providence. When hostilities ended in November 1918 and regular sailings could be resumed, the expectations of both the company and the city rose once again. Unfortunately, these sanguine hopes did not materialize. Congressional action, provoked by a wave of xenophobia that swept the nation during the years following the war, led to both selective and restrictive immigration acts that seriously reduced the line's passenger traffic, the mainstay of its operations at Providence.

Fore and Aft

The steamship company attempted to counter this adverse situation by expanding its sailings in the early 1920s to include various ports in the eastern Mediterranean and Black Sea along with its already established sailings to Portugal, the Azores and Italy. The line also attempted, unsuccessfully, to court tourist traffic to and from Europe.

Throughout the whole of its stay in Providence, the Fabre Line failed to develop any significant cargo traffic at the port. The *Providence Journal*, the board of trade and the chamber of commerce, staunch supporters of the company, lent their efforts toward convincing local businessmen that cargo could be shipped more cheaply through the port of Providence than through New York. Their efforts were unsuccessful, and the line's cargo handling at Providence always remained scanty.

The great worldwide depression of the 1930s sounded the death knell for the Fabre Line at Providence, where passenger traffic dwindled to a trickle after 1931. The termination of Fabre operations at Providence came unannounced and without recognition on July 4, 1934, when the *Sinaia*, eastward bound from New York, made the company's final call. The local press gave no indication that this was Fabre's last visit to the Ocean State. However, those who followed the company's operations must have suspected that the line's termination at Providence was near at hand. The *Sinaia* sailed down Narragansett Bay on that July holiday, taking with it twenty-three years of transatlantic steamship service from Providence.

The Fabre Line had provided the port of Providence with its first and only significant transatlantic maritime involvement. Hopes had been high during the spring of 1919 that Providence would develop into a major Atlantic seaport, yet the established strength of the port of New York crushed these hopes. Immigrant legislation of the 1920s and the Great Depression in the 1930s ended the company's stay at Providence.

In 1937, even the famous Long Island Sound steamers, so well known to those living along the shores of Narragansett and Mount Hope Bays, ceased to operate. Both the Providence Line and the legendary Fall River Line also steamed into history and sold their ships for scrap, the victims of the automobile, the truck and changing times. In 1942, the Colonial Line, which ran the only surviving Long Island Sound steamers out of Narragansett Bay, terminated operations when its vessels were commandeered for war service by the national government. Its sleek steamer *Arrow* closed out overnight passenger service from Providence to New York via Long Island Sound on March 29, 1942.

Subsequent maritime traffic at the port of Providence, devastated by the 1938 hurricane, was reduced to bulk carriers and a rare cruise ship coming up the bay, a situation that continued until 2007, when American Cruise Line began to visit Dock Conley, just a few hundred feet north of State Pier Number 1. Since then, its small luxury ships have used Providence as a point of embarkation and debarkation for weekly summer excursions along the southern New England coast.

During its twenty-three-year tenure, Fabre liners carried around eighty-four thousand alien immigrants to Providence, of which some eleven thousand chose Rhode Island as their permanent residence. State Pier Number 1, Rhode Island's Ellis Island, is now a facility used exclusively for the export of scrap metal—what poetess Emma Lazarus might call "the wretched refuse of our teeming shore"—and all of Fabre's visiting ships have been scrapped as well. *Sic transit gloria mundi.*

Although the days of transatlantic glory along the Providence waterfront came to an end in the summer of 1934, the Fabre Line left an enduring legacy. No other single factor in Rhode Island's history is more responsible for the state's cultural and ethnoreligious diversity, and the descendants of its "alien arrivals" will continue to shape Rhode Island's course now and into the future.

On April 1, 2007, coauthors Patrick Conley (left) and former Rhode Island Supreme Court associate justice Robert Flanders presented their new book, *The Rhode Island Constitution: A Reference Guide*. It was the first of sixty books (and sixty lectures) presented by the Fabre Line Club (the educational and cultural outreach arm of the Rhode Island Publications Society) from its foundation in February 2007 until its termination in December 2013. A Fabre Line poster serves as a backdrop to the podium. The stone fireplace to which it is attached is topped by a large colorful replica of a Fabre Line steamship funnel. This history of Providence and the Fabre Line will be presented to club members (which over seven years included more than five hundred individuals) on December 17, 2013, the 100th anniversary of the arrival of the *Venezia*, the first Fabre liner to dock at adjacent State Pier Number 1. Because the city literally scrapped its expensive plans to develop the Allens Avenue waterfront, this book's presentation will be the Fabre Line Club's final event. *Conley Collection.*

APPENDIX

The information in Tables 1 through 3 was found in the *Annual Report of the Commissioner General of Immigration for the Fiscal Year*. Table 1 lists the totals for passenger traffic to and from the Port of Providence for the years 1906 to 1932. It is divided into the broad categories of aliens and U.S. citizens admitted and departed annually, along with other subdivisions. Table 2 indicates the intended future residence of immigrant aliens who entered the United States through the Port of Providence and is broken down by state for the years 1915 to 1932. Table 3 lists the ports of destination for passengers and their numbers departing from the United States via the Fabre vessels from the Ports of New York and Providence from 1911 to 1920. It is broken down into the broad categories of aliens and citizens by years.

Table 4, compiled from the "Record of Entrances and Clearances of Vessels Engaged in Foreign Trade, Port of Providence" for the years 1911–32. Arrivals and departures are listed by date of entry or departure to or from Providence.

Table 5 gives information concerning the construction, career and destruction of the eleven Fabre Line passenger vessels that visited Providence.

TABLE 1
Total Passenger Traffic to and from the Port of Providence

YEAR	ALIENS ADMITTED					ALIENS DEBARRED	TOTAL ADMITTED	EMIGRANT	NON-EMIGRANT	ALIENS DEPORTED				TOTAL DEPARTED
	IMMIGRANT	NONIMMIGRANT	TOTAL		U.S. CITIZENS					TOTAL	U.S. CITIZENS		ALIENS DEPARTED	
1906	-	-	19		-	-	19	-	-	-	-		-	-
1907	-	-	0		-	-	0	-	-	-	-		-	-
1908	-	-	0		-	-	0	-	-	-	-		-	-
1909	68	-	68		-	-	68	32	-	32	-		-	32
1910	48	-	48		2	2	52	-	3	3	3		-	6
1911	266	119	385		77	2	464	164	36	200	104		0	304
1912	5,178	692	5,870		413	63	6,346	1,517	503	2,020	219		1	2,240
1913	11,101	1,002	12,103		533	100	12,736	1,605	644	2,341	444		10	2,795
1914	9,852	970	10,822		483	173	11,478	1,264	1,028	2,292	538		9	2,839
1915	2,536	240	2,776		223	33	3,032	1,984	518	2,502	413		11	2,926
1916	4,029	218	4,247		209	26	4,482	845	330	1,175	240		9	1,424
1917	5,070	122	5,172		212	36	5,420	447	137	584	119		4	707
1918	1,351	35	1,381		82	9	1,472	0	0	0	0		1	0
1919	367	3	370		24	3	397	503	52	555	152		6	713
1920	8,213	103	8,315		470	10	8,795	3,654	460	4,114	1,446		3	5,563
1921	12,860	440	13,300		520	69	13,889	3,614	359	3,973	1,265		11	5,249
1922	2,010	432	2,442		521	161	3,124	3,060	224	3,284	928		20	4,232
1923	2,834	758	3,592		533	172	4,307	1,404	248	1,652	624		8	2,284
1924	7,347	2,600	9,947		1,599	90	11,636	1,346	216	1,562	449		24	2,035
1925	948	1,489	2,437		1,236	21	3,694	1,274	394	1,668	441		26	2,135
1926	1,214	1,861	3,075		1,593	5	4,673	1,026	403	1,429	457		32	1,918
1927	1,659	2,188	3,847		1,839	24	5,700	659	272	931	465		23	1,419
1928	2,064	2,273	4,337		2,170	19	6,526	236	705	941	427		23	1,391
1929	1,719	1,777	3,496		1,893	23	5,412	341	386	727	430		34	1,191
1930	1,511	1,469	2,980		1,845	16	4,841	0	709	709	345		42	1,096
1931	928	1,085	2,013		1,425	13	3,451	24	743	767	376		35	1,178
1932	369	436	805		679	3	1,487	86	530	616	323		50	989

*Compiled from "Table I–Aliens admitted, departed, debarred, and deported, and United States citizens arrived and departed, fiscal years ended June 30, 1907-1932, by ports," found in the *Annual Reports* from 1907 to 1932. After 1932, the *Annual Reports* is published only in condensed form.

TABLE 2
State of Intended Future Residence of Immigrant Aliens Admitted at the Port of Providence

YEAR	TOTAL	CALIFORNIA	CONNECTICUT	ILLINOIS	MASSACHUSETTS	NEW JERSEY	NEW YORK	OHIO	PENNSYLVANIA	RHODE ISLAND
1915	2,536	674	27	28	1,113	14	118	17	31	425
1916	4,029	506	30	5	2,780	3	122	1	58	499
1917	5,070	383	97	10	3,468	13	98	1	69	883
1918	1,351	172	58	3	795	5	29	1	46	232
1919	367	27	12	3	241	0	10	0	2	51
1920	8,213	1,131	377	23	4,309	156	423	44	205	1,450
1921	12,860	1,319	812	182	5,434	463	1,219	346	366	2,328
1922	2,010	347	80	147	526	44	413	42	98	164
1923	2,834	407	114	72	884	273	472	28	128	277
1924	7,347	397	212	198	1,505	422	2,632	208	661	515
1925	948	108	19	24	208	95	243	22	69	64
1926	1,214	124	30	47	217	66	314	50	109	107
1927	1,659	45	37	84	214	56	589	88	218	109
1928	2,064	75	80	96	320	70	796	79	168	168
1929	1,719	86	57	88	248	116	636	55	119	111
1930	1,511	41	55	67	284	87	522	38	84	140
1931	928	81	35	28	267	32	227	22	52	104
1932	369	52	28	16	68	14	94	5	13	34

Compiled from "Table XI-B: Immigrant aliens admitted during fiscal year ended June 30, 1915–1932, by States of Intended Future Residence and Ports of Entry," found in the *Annual Reports* from 1915 to 1932.

Table 3
Passengers Departed from the United States Via Fabre Line Vessels Through the Ports of New York and Providence

From	To	Year	Aliens	Citizens	Total
New York	Genoa	1911	1		1
	Harve		1		1
	Lisbon		8	6	14
	Marseilles		150	196	346
	Messina		1		1
	Naples		9,642	1,052	10,694
	Palermo		4		4
	Piraeus		3		3
	Villefranche			12	12
	Azores		437	143	580
Providence	Lisbon	1911	6	12	18
	Azores		94	83	177
New York	Lisbon	1912	168	31	199
	Marseilles		569	410	979
	Messina		12		12
	Naples		14,132	1,493	15,625
	Palermo		5		5
	Villefranche			4	4
	Azores		269	94	363
	Miscellaneous		3	15	18
Providence	Lisbon	1912	183	11	194
	Marseilles		24	11	35

From	To	Year	Aliens	Citizens	Total
	Naples		1,367	42	1,409
	Azores		424	155	579
New York	Lisbon	1913	204	32	236
	Marseilles		5,855	488	6,343
	Naples		9,606	1,839	11,445
	Patras, Greece		3,721	43	3,764
	Spain		6	9	15
	Villefranche		13	44	57
	Algiers		4	11	15
	Azores		127	48	175
Providence	Lisbon	1913	281	31	312
	Marseilles		274	62	336
	Naples		1,171	132	1,306
	Azores		520	219	739
New York	Lisbon	1914	190	36	226
	Marseilles		493	551	1,044
	Naples		12,675	2,444	15,119
	Spain		27	16	43
	Villefranche		6	39	45
	Algiers		5	20	25
Providence	Lisbon	1914	521	111	632
	Marseilles		24	15	39
	Naples		1,062	131	1,193
	Azores		685	281	966

From	To	Year	Aliens	Citizens	Total
New York	Lisbon	1915	350	23	373
	Marseilles		1,915	404	2,319
	Naples		9,876	1,281	11,157
	Spain		410	15	425
	Azores		476	76	552
Providence	Lisbon	1915	682	37	719
	Marseilles		5	28	33
	Naples		1,250	131	1,381
	Spain		5	6	11
	Azores		560	211	771
New York	Lisbon	1916	299	32	331
	Marseilles		82	60	142
	Naples		8,810	328	9,138
	Spain		29	4	33
	Azores		133	51	184
Providence	Lisbon	1916	477	42	519
	Azores		698	198	896
New York	Azores	1917	168	43	211
	Lisbon		211	26	237
	Marseilles		34	3	37
	Naples		367	46	413
Providence	Azores	1917	153	41	194
	Horta, Azores		28	11	39
	Lisbon		353	40	393

From	To	Year	Aliens	Citizens	Total
	Ponta Delgada, Azores		50	27	77
New York	Azores	1918	1,528	149	1,677
	Bordeaux		294	10	304
	Lisbon		291	9	300
	Marseilles		58	15	73
Providence	Not Listed	1918			
New York	Azores	1919	577	126	703
	Lisbon		1,505	110	1,617
	Marseilles		4,818	311	5,129
	Piraeus		1,881	97	1,978
Providence	Angra, Azores	1919	21	9	30
	Horta, Azores		7	6	13
	Ponta Delgada, Azores		268	51	221
	Lisbon		259	86	264
New York	Azores	1920	373	179	552
	Constantinople		826	13	839
	Lisbon		510	141	651
	Madeira		191	35	226
	Marseilles		1,752	492	2,244
	Miscellaneous		258	89	347
	Naples		8,416	1,723	10,139

From	To	Year	Aliens	Citizens	Total
	Palermo		3,110	829	3,939
	Piraeus		5,146	1,051	6,197
	Spain		91	29	120
	Trieste		332	49	381
Providence	Angra, Azores	1920	541	204	745
	Horta, Azores		340	203	543
	Ponta Delgada, Azores		1,461	524	1,985
	St. Michael's, Azores		200	108	308
	Lisbon		1,193	357	1,550
	Madeira		121	21	142
	Marseilles		191	26	217

Compiled from "Table XXIII: Passengers Departed from the United States, Fiscal Years Ended June 30, 1911–1920," found in the *Annual Reports* from 1911 to 1920.

Table 4
Transatlantic Arrivals and Departure of Fabre Vessels at the Port of Providence

Date	Arrivals	Departures
1911		
May 13		*Madonna*
June 16	*Madonna*	
July 1	*Germania*	
August 1	*Madonna*	
August 10		*Madonna*
August 14	*Germania*	
September 9	*Roma*	
September 16		*Roma*
September 26	*Venezia*	
October 11		*Germania*
October 21	*Roma*	
November 3	*Madonna*	
November 18		*Venezia*
November 21	*Germania*	
December 9		*Roma*
December 23	*Madonna*	
December 30		*Madonna*
1912		
January 8	*Germania*	
January 27	*Roma*	
February 9	*Madonna*	
February 24	*Germania*	
March 1		*Germania*
March 14	*Roma*	
March 22	*Madonna*	
March 22		*Roma*

Date	Arrivals	Departures
April 6	*Germania*	
April 14		*Germania*
April 28	*Roma*	
May 7		*Roma*
May 8	*Madonna*	
May 14		*Madonna*
May 19	*Germania*	
May 29		*Germania*
May 31	*Venezia*	
June 13	*Roma*	
June 20		*Roma*
July 2	*Madonna*	
July 12		*Madonna*
July 14	*Venezia*	
July 27	*Roma*	
July 30		*Venezia*
August 6		*Roma*
August 17	*Madonna*	
August 23		*Madonna*
August 30	*Venezia*	
September 12	*Roma*	
September 19		*Roma*
October 2	*Madonna*	
October 8		*Madonna*
October 14	*Venezia*	
October 20		*Venezia*
October 25	*Roma*	
November 2		*Roma*
November 24	*Germania*	
November 29	*Venezia*	

DATE	ARRIVALS	DEPARTURES
November 30		*Germania*
December 5		*Venezia*
December 9	*Roma*	
1913		
January 5	*Madonna*	
January 10	*Germania*	
January 19	*Venezia*	
February 5	*Roma*	
February 15		*Roma*
February 28	*Germania*	
March 8		*Germania*
March 19	*Venezia*	
March 21	*Roma*	
April 1		*Roma*
April 18	*Germania*	
April 22	*Madonna*	
May 3	*Venezia*	
May 6	*Roma*	
May 17		*Roma*
May 30	*Madonna*	
June 1	*Germania*	
June 5		*Madonna*
June 11		*Germania*
June 16	*Venezia*	
June 22	*Roma*	
June 25		*Venezia*
July 1		*Roma*
July 12	*Madonna*	
July 20		*Madonna*
August 1	*Venezia*	

Date	Arrivals	Departures
August 6	*Roma*	
August 7		*Venezia*
August 16		*Roma*
August 27 or 28	*Madonna*	
September 4		*Madonna*
September 20	*Roma*	
September 24		*Venezia*
October 1		*Roma*
October 13	*Madonna*	
October 16	*Germania*	
October 25		*Germania*
November 6	*Roma*	
November 13		*Roma*
November 25	*Madonna*	
November 30	*Germania*	
December 3		*Madonna*
December 17	*Venezia*	
1914		
January 4	*Roma*	
January 19	*Madonna*	
January 24		*Madonna*
February 17	*Roma*	
March 5	*Madonna*	
March 6	*Germania*	
March 12		*Germania*
March 25	*Venezia*	
April 7		*Roma*
April 7	*Germania*	
April 15	*Madonna*	
April 22		*Madonna*

Date	Arrivals	Departures
April 24	*Roma*	
April 29		*Roma*
May 4	*Venezia*	
May 17	*Germania*	
May 23		*Germania*
May 28	*Madonna*	
June 3	*Roma*	
June 6		*Madonna*
June 11		*Roma*
June 20	*Venezia*	
June 26		*Venezia*
June 27	*Germania*	
July 8		*Germania*
July 14	*Madonna*	
July 19	*Roma*	
July 21		*Madonna*
July 25		*Roma*
August 15	*Germania*	
September (None)		
October 5	*Roma*	
October 15		*Roma*
October 21		*Madonna*
October 22	**Britannia*	
October 28		*Britannia*
November 5	*Venezia*	
November 13		*Venezia*
November 19	*Roma*	
November 28		*Roma*
November 30	*Madonna*	
December 5	*Britannia*	

Date	Arrivals	Departures
December 9		*Madonna*
December 12		*Britannia*
1915		
January 8	*Venezia*	
January 20		*Roma*
January 23	*Madonna*	
February (None)		
March 4	*Roma*	
March 10	*Madonna*	
March 10		*Roma*
April 18	*Roma*	
April 27		*Roma*
April 28	*Madonna*	
May 7		*Madonna*
June 1	*Roma*	
June 9		*Roma*
June 17	*Venezia*	
July 17	*Roma*	
July 27		*Roma*
August (None)		
September 1	*Roma*	
September 9		*Roma*
October 15	*Roma*	
October 23		*Roma*
November 29	*Roma*	
December 8		*Roma*
1916		
January 17	*Roma*	
January 24		*Roma*
February 24	*Roma*	

DATE	ARRIVALS	DEPARTURES
March 5		*Roma*
April 3	*Roma*	
May 13	*Roma*	
June (None)		
July 10	*Roma*	
July 19		*Roma*
August 30	*Roma*	
September 9		*Roma*
October 23	*Roma*	
November 1		*Roma*
December 23	*Roma*	
1917		
January 8		*Roma*
February 10	*Roma*	
March 24	*Roma*	
April (None)		
May 2	*Roma*	
June (None)		
July (None)		
August 6	*Roma*	
September (None)		
October 7	*Roma*	
November (None)		
December 5	*Roma*	
1918		
January (None)		
February (None)		
March (None)		
April 21	*Roma*	
May (None)		

Date	Arrivals	Departures
June (None)		
July (None)		
August (None)		
September (None)		
October (None)		
November (None)		
December (None)		
1919		
January (None)		
February (None)		
March (None)		
April 10	*Britannia*	
April 22		*Britannia*
May (None)		
June 19		*Britannia*
July 26		*Roma*
July 26	*Canada*	
August 13		*Britannia*
September 9	*Roma*	
September 17		*Roma*
October 14	*Britannia*	
October 29		*Britannia*
November 19		*Roma*
December 19		*Britannia*
December 20	*Canada*	
1920		
January (None)		
February 2	*Roma*	
February 19	*Britannia*	
March 24	*Roma*	

Date	Arrivals	Departures
April 1		*Roma*
April 10	*Britannia*	
May 12	*Roma*	
May 22		*Roma*
June 9	*Britannia*	
June 16		*Britannia*
June 19	*Providence*	
July 1	*Roma*	
July 2		*Providence*
July 19		*Roma*
July 26	*Britannia*	
August 5		*Britannia*
August 7	*Canada*	
August 22	*Roma*	
September 1		*Roma*
September 1	*Britannia*	
September 11		*Madonna*
September 15		*Britannia*
October 5	*Asia*	
October 13		*Canada*
October 19		*Roma*
October 27	*Britannia*	
November 5		*Madonna*
November 22	*Roma*	
December 1		*Roma*
December 9	*Asia*	
December 13	*Canada*	
December 15		*Britannia*
December 30		*Madonna*

DATE	ARRIVALS	DEPARTURES
1921		
January 15		*Braga*
January 27	*Braga*	
February 5		*Britannia*
February 14	*Asia*	
February 22		*Asia*
March 4	*Britannia*	
March 5		*Canada*
March 17		*Braga*
April 6	*Britannia*	
April 17		*Britannia*
April 29		*Canada*
April 29	*Braga*	
May 6		*Asia*
May 14		*Braga*
May 26	*Britannia*	
June 8		*Britannia*
June 18		*Canada*
June 20	*Asia*	
July 1		*Asia*
July 10	*Roma*	
July 21		*Roma*
July 27	*Canada*	
August 5		*Canada*
August 27	*Asia*	
September 8		*Asia*
September 16		*Providence*
September 16	*Roma*	
September 27		*Roma*
October 6		*Braga*

DATE	ARRIVALS	DEPARTURES
October 8	*Canada*	
October 19		*Canada*
October 22		*Britannia*
November 12	*Roma*	
November 12		*Roma*
November 16		*Asia*
December 7		*Canada*
December 13		*Braga*
December 21		*Britannia*
1922		
January 7	*Roma*	
January 19		*Roma*
February 5		*Canada*
February 13	*Asia*	
February 22		*Asia*
March 6	*Braga*	
March 16		*Braga*
March 25	*Canada*	
April 7		*Canada*
April 25	*Asia*	
May 5		*Asia*
May 21	*Canada*	
June 19	*Braga*	
July 1	*Roma*	
July 26	*Asia*	
July 26		*Asia*
August 1	*Canada*	
August 11		*Canada*
September 1	*Braga*	
September 12		*Braga*

Date	**Arrivals**	**Departures**
September 30		*Roma*
October 1	*Britannia*	
October 13		*Britannia*
October 19		*Asia*
November 1	*Canada*	
November 10		*Madonna*
December 2	*Roma*	
December 12		*Roma*
1923		
January 2	*Asia*	
January 10		*Canada*
January 14		*Asia*
February 2	*Roma*	
February 16		*Roma*
March 15		*Braga*
April 2	*Asia*	
April 12		*Asia*
May 1	*Britannia*	
May 2		*Canada*
June 3	*Asia*	
June 15		*Asia*
July 2	*Britannia*	
July 12		*Canada*
July 12		*Britannia*
July 29		*Patria*
August 1	*Roma*	
September 1	*Asia*	
September 11		*Asia*
September 11	*Patria*	
October 1	*Canada*	

DATE	ARRIVALS	DEPARTURES
October 1	*Roma*	
October 10		*Roma* (sailing canceled)
October 11		*Canada*
October 19	*Britannia*	
October 26		*Britannia*
November 1	*Madonna*	
November 2	*Asia*	
November 13		*Asia* (Cape Verde Islands)
November 23		*Roma*
December 3	*Britannia*	
December 12		*Britannia*
1924		
January 4	*Canada*	
January 11		*Canada*
February 11	*Asia*	
February 22		*Asia*
March 3	*Madonna*	
March 13		*Madonna*
March 13	*Patria*	
April 4	*Braga*	
April 13		*Braga*
May 7	*Asia*	
May 15		*Asia*
May 31	*Madonna*	
June 29	*Braga*	
June 30	*Roma*	
July 11		*Roma*
July 23		*Britannia*
August 2	*Asia*	
August 9		*Asia*

Date	Arrivals	Departures
August 27	*Canada*	
August 27		*Canada*
August 31	*Madonna*	
September 15	*Britannia*	
September 25		*Britannia*
October 2	*Braga*	
October 10		*Braga*
October 22	*Roma*	
November 3	*Sinaia*	
November 13		*Sinaia*
November 13	*Canada*	
November 22		*Canada*
November 22	*Britannia*	
December 3		*Britannia*
December 11		*Asia*
December 31	*Madonna*	
1925		
January 8	*Roma*	
January 10		*Madonna*
January 20		*Roma*
February 3	*Braga*	
February 14		*Braga*
February 16	*Britannia*	
February 25		*Britannia*
March 2	*Canada*	
March 12		*Asia*
March 31	*Madonna*	
April (None)		
May 7	*Braga*	
May 15		*Braga*

Date	Arrivals	Departures
May 20	*Britannia*	
May 30		*Britannia*
June 12		*Asia*
June 28	*Sinaia*	
July 3	*Roma*	
July 8		*Sinaia*
July 16		*Roma*
July 25	*Britannia*	
August 4		*Britannia*
August 20	*Canada*	
August 29		*Canada*
September 10		*Asia*
September 12	*Roma*	
September 23		*Roma*
October 1	*Sinaia*	
October 5	*Providence*	
October 10		*Sinaia*
October 15	*Britannia*	
October 22		*Britannia* (Cape Verde Islands)
November 4	*Braga*	
November 12		*Braga*
December 1	*Canada*	
December 12		*Canada*
1926		
January 4	*Roma*	
January 14		*Roma*
February 13	*Britannia*	
February 21		*Britannia*
March 4	*Braga*	
March 13		*Braga*

Date	Arrivals	Departures
March 14	*Roma*	
March 26		*Roma*
April 5	*Sinaia*	
April 13		*Sinaia*
April 30	*Asia*	
May 9		*Asia*
May 31	*Roma*	
June 6	*Braga*	
June 15		*Braga*
July 4	*Sinaia*	
July 14		*Sinaia*
July 31	*Asia*	
August 10		*Asia*
August 23	*Canada*	
September 2		*Canada*
September 6	*Braga*	
September 17		*Braga*
October 4	*Sinaia*	
October 10	*Roma*	
October 14		*Sinaia*
October 20		*Roma* (Cape Verde Islands)
November 10	*Asia*	
November 20		*Asia*
December 18	*Roma*	
December 30		*Roma*
December 31	*Sinaia*	
1927		
January 11		*Sinaia*
February 27	*Asia*	
March 10		*Asia*

Date	Arrivals	Departures
March 30	*Roma*	
March 31	*Patria*	
April 12		*Roma*
April 27	*Sinaia*	
May 7		*Sinaia*
May 9	*Providence*	
May 30	*Asia*	
June 8		*Asia*
June 10	*Patria*	
July 1	*Roma*	
July 8	*Providence*	
July 13		*Roma*
July 30	*Sinaia*	
August 9	*Patria*	
August 22	*Canada*	
August 31	*Providence*	
September 1	*Asia*	
September 2		*Canada*
October 2	*Patria*	
October 6	*Roma*	
October 30		*Roma* (Cape Verde Islands)
November 3	*Sinaia*	
November 12		*Sinaia*
November 12	*Providence*	
December 6	*Asia*	
December 14		*Providence*
1928		
January 1	*Canada*	
January 11		*Canada*
January 27	*Providence*	

Date	Arrivals	Departures
February (None)		
March 2	*Patria*	
March 12	*Sinaia*	
April 8	*Providence*	
April 20		*Asia*
May 11	*Roma*	
May 16	*Patria*	
May 19		*Roma*
June 7	*Sinaia*	
June 16		*Sinaia*
June 23	*Providence*	
July 11	*Asia*	
July 17	*Patria*	
July 21		*Asia*
August 9	*Alesia*	
August 17		*Alesia*
August 17	*Canada*	
August 28	*Providence*	
August 30		*Canada*
September 12	*Sinaia*	
September 16	*Patria*	
October 16	*Asia*	
October 24		*Asia*
November 7	*Alesia*	
November 14	*Providence*	
November 18		*Alesia*
November 26	*Patria*	
December 14	*Sinaia*	
1929		
January 23	*Providence*	

DATE	ARRIVALS	DEPARTURES
February 8	*Asia*	
February 17		*Asia*
March 10	*Alesia*	
March 19		*Alesia*
April 6	*Sinaia*	
April 17		*Sinaia*
May 4	*Patria*	
May 13	*Asia*	
May 21		*Asia*
June 9	*Alesia*	
June 19		*Alesia*
June 23	*Providence*	
August 9	*Asia*	
August 20		*Asia*
August 21	*Providence*	
September 11	*Alesia*	
September 14	*Patria*	
September 19		*Alesia*
October 12	*Sinaia*	
October 22		*Sinaia*
November 10	*Asia*	
November 13	*Providence*	
November 22		*Asia*
November 26	*Patria*	
November	*Sevenitas* (cargo vessel)	
December 14	*Alesia*	
1930		
January 22	*Providence*	
February 12	*Patria*	
March 14	*Alesia*	

DATE	ARRIVALS	DEPARTURES
March 22		*Alesia*
April 6	*Providence*	
April 27	*Sinaia*	
April 28	*Patria*	
May 4		*Sinaia*
June 10	*Alesia*	
June 20		*Alesia*
June 20	*Providence*	
July 18	*Sinaia*	
July 18	*Patria*	
July 27		*Sinaia*
August 22	*Providence*	
September 4	*Alesia*	
September 11	*Patria*	
September 17		*Alesia*
October 14	*Sinaia*	
October 24		*Sinaia*
November 13	*Providence*	
November 29	*Patria*	
December 4	*Alesia*	
December 11		*Alesia*
1931		
January (None)		
February 2	*Providence*	
February 12	*Sinaia*	
February 21		*Sinaia*
February 24	*Patria*	
March (None)		
April 2	*Providence*	
April 18	*Sinaia*	

Date	Arrivals	Departures
April 24		*Sinaia*
May 12	*Patria*	
June 20	*Providence*	
July 14	*Sinaia*	
July 24		*Sinaia*
August 25	*Providence*	
September (None)		
October 15	*Sinaia*	
October 23		*Sinaia*
November 25	*Providence*	
December (None)		
1932		
January 6	*Sinaia*	
January 17		*Sinaia*
February (None)		
March 22	*Sinaia*	
March 30		*Sinaia*
April (None)		
May 25	*Sinaia*	
June 3		*Sinaia*
July 21		*Canada*
August 8	*Sinaia*	
August 17		*Sinaia*
September 17	*Rochambeau* (charter)	*Rochambeau* (charter)
October 23		*Sinaia*
November 29	*Sinaia*	
December 4		*Sinaia*
1933		
January (None)		
February (None)		

Date	Arrivals	Departures
March (None)		
April 14	Sinaia	
April 23		Sinaia
May (None)		
June 23	Sinaia	
July 2		Sinaia
August 25		Sinaia
September (None)		
October 20	Sinaia	
October 29		Sinaia
November (None)		
December (None)		
1934		
January (None)		
February (None)		
March 21	Sinaia	
March 28		Sinaia
April (None)		
May 9	Sinaia	
May 16		Sinaia
June 26	Sinaia	
July 4		Sinaia

The Fabre Line terminated activities at the Port of Providence after July 1934.
Compiled from the Record of Entrance and Clearances for the years 1911 to 1934.
*Formerly the *Germania*

TABLE 5
THE CONSTRUCTION, CAREER AND DESTRUCTION OF THE ELEVEN FABRE LINE PASSENGER VESSELS TO VISIT PROVIDENCE

Name	Date Built	Place Built	Gross Tonnage & Length	Service	Ultimate Fate
Madonna	1905	England	5,663 and 430	Transatlantic (1905–25) West Africa (1927–34)	Scrapped in Italy (May 1934)
Brittania (Germania)	1903	Port de Bouc, France	5,103 and 407	Transatlantic (1911–26)	Scrapped at La Seyne, France (1927)
Roma	1902	La Seyne, France	5,671 and 411	Transatlantic (1911–28)	Scrapped at La Seyne, France (1928)
Venezia	1907	Wallsend-on-Tyne, England	6,707 and 457	Transatlantic (1907–15); chartered to Cie Generale Transatlantique (1919)	Desetroyed by fire in the North Atlantic (October 1919) while under charter to the French Line
Canada	1911	La Seyne, France	9,684 and 476	Transatlantic (1919–28); transferred to West African service (1930–52)	Scrapped in Newport, Wales (1952)
Providence	1914 (dedication) 1920 (maiden voyage)	La Seyne, France	11,900 and 489	Transatlantic (1920–31); chartered to Messageries Maritimes in 1932 and sold to MM in 1940; eastern Mediterranean Service (1945-51)	Scrapped at LaSpezia, Italy (1951)
Asia (Alice)	1907	Glasgow Scotland	6,122 and 415	Built for Austrian firm of Unione Austriaca of Trieste; seized by Brazilian navy (1917); war reparation from Austria to Brazil; purchased by the Fabre Line (1920); transatlantic (1920–29); Mediterranean-African run (1930)	Destroyed by fire in Red Sea while carrying Muslim pilgrims to Mecca (May 1930)

Name	Date Built	Place Built	Gross Tonnage & Length	Service	Ultimate Fate
Braga (Laura)	1907	Glasgow, Scotland	6,122 and 415	Built for Austrian firm of Unione Austriaca of Trieste; seized by Brazilian navy (1917); war reparation from Austria to Brazil; purchased by the Fabre Line (1920); transatlantic (1921–26); Mediterranean-African run (1930)	Wrecked in the Aegean Sea off the Greek island of Aspra (November 1926)
Patria	1913	La Seyne, France	11,885 and 487	Transatlantic (1914–31); chartered to Messageries Maritimes in 1932, sold to MM in 1940 and acquired by the British Steam Navigation Company	Sunk by three explosions in Haifa Harbor (November 1940). The wreck was scrapped in 1952.
Sinaia	1924	Glasgow, Scotland	8,567 and 439	Transatlantic (1925–34), then cargo only	Seized by Germany (1942) for use as a hospital ship. Scuttled in Marseilles by the Germans as a war measure (1944); raised by the French and scrapped (1946)
Alesia (Montreal, Konig Freidrich August)	1906	Hamburg, Germany	9,720 and 476	War reparation from Germany to England; sold to Canadian Pacific Railroad (1921) and renamed Montreal; sold to Fabre Line (1928) and	Scrapped at Genoa, Italy (1933)

NOTES

CHAPTER 1

1. For a glimpse of Providence during the first three decades of the twentieth century, see Conley and Campbell, *Providence*, 143–78. See also Geake, *History* for a long view of this short river. The level of optimism for the city's future prompted the publication in 1909 of a volume of scholarly essays dealing with various aspects of Providence life and its prospects for further development; see Kirk, *Modern City*.
2. *Providence Journal*, September 1–3, 1910; hereafter cited as *Journal*.
3. Numerous references to the proposal appeared in the *Journal* and *Providence* magazines from time to time.
4. A similar situation existed at the port of New York roughly between 1900 and 1910. See Taylor, *Productive Monopoly*, 137.
5. Carroll, *Rhode Island*, 2:303.
6. See Bonsor, *North Atlantic*, 342–4, 383; Bois, *Armements*; Gibbs, *Passenger Liners*, 341–2. Fabre vessels all maintained accommodations for more than forty first-cabin passengers after 1902 and until passenger service to Providence was terminated during the Depression years.
7. Taylor, *Productive Monopoly*, 138.
8. Ibid., 131–41; Farrelly, interviewed by Conley and Smith, August 31, 1972; Farelly, interviewed by Jennings, July 17, 1974 (hereafter cited as Farelly); O'Neil, interviewed by Jennings, July 17 and 19, 1974

(hereafter cited as O'Neil). Both Farrelly and O'Neil were longtime employees of the U.S. Customs Service. Farrelly began his career in Providence in 1919 as an inspector and served in various capacities at the port until 1930; he retired with the title of deputy collector of the port of New York. O'Neil worked in connection with the New York waterfront in 1919; he began in the customs service in Providence in 1924 and remained there until his retirement in 1965 with the title of deputy collector. Both men remember the congestion at New York vividly; O'Neil recalls seeing horse-drawn carts lined up for blocks at the terminals waiting to be unloaded.

9. Taylor, *Productive Monopoly*, 137.
10. The literature on American immigration and ethnicity is voluminous. The best reference work is Climent, *Encyclopedia*, see especially 1:97–132; Jones, *American Immigration* is a good (though dated) general survey. On the "new" immigration, consult Bodner, *Transplanted*; Higham, *Strangers*; and Nugent, *Crossings*.
11. *Book of Rhode Island*, 270; *Journal*, May 25, 1911. The Fabre Line had attractive offers to locate at other New England cities such as Boston, Lynn and New London.
12. Carroll, *Rhode Island*, 2:85. It is interesting that while studying the effect of railroad control of the New England coastal steamboat lines forty years later, W.L. Taylor drew essentially the same conclusion about the essential benefit of the New Haven's monopoly.
13. Carroll, *Rhode Island*, 849–50; *Journal*, 1909–1915, passim. Weller, *New Haven* outlines the history of this transportation monopoly; Lowenthal *Titanic Railroad* is a fascinating, well-illustrated account of this brainchild of Charles Hays; see also, Patten, "Railroad," *Rhode Island*, H 140–45; and a recent survey of the state's railroad history in Heppner, *Railroads*.
14. Farrelly; O'Neil; *Journal*, passim; Connelly, interviewed by Jennings, July 11, 1974 (hereafter cited as Connelly); Nelson, interviewed by Jennings, July 10, 1974 (hereafter cited as Nelson). Connelly was a senior official with the customs service in Providence; Nelson was the president of Goff & Page, Inc., former local steamship agents of the Fabre Line.
15. Farrelly; O'Neil; Nelson; *Journal*, passim. A good description of the scams perpetrated against these immigrants is contained in Taylor, *Distant Magnet*, 145–66.
16. Naples was thought to be the intended terminal of the line, and the announcement that the vessels would sail from Marseilles came as a disappointment to Italian interests. The *Journal*, on May 8, 1911,

disclosed that "the reason for the change from Naples to Marseilles… is explained by the fact that there is at present a lack of available steamers on the direct Italian lines." Our interpretation here is that the Fabre Line did not have enough steamers plying between Italian ports and New York to divert any to a direct Providence run. The line must have thought that sailings between Providence and Italian ports would be self-sustaining and not requiring continuing on to New York to obtain a full cargo. Interestingly enough, the lifeline of the company at Providence proved to be passengers, and the majority embarked at Portuguese ports such as Lisbon and the islands of Cape Verde, Madeira and the Azores.
17. *Journal*, May 7–8, 1911.
18. Ibid., May 8, 1911.
19. Will B. Thayer was the comedic writer; *Journal*, March 18, 1911.
20. *Journal*, March 24, 1911. When the railroad gave the Fabre Line permission to use the facilities where its steamboats docked, the New Haven stipulated that the Fabre Line was not to handle freight at this wharf.
21. Ibid., March 25, 1911. This schedule was confirmed by Elwell & Company a month later, *Journal*, April 21, 1911.
22. *Journal*, May 14, 1911; Rose, *Block Island*, 104–17. "Maizie," the author of a colorful book on Block Island's past, has an account of Tal Dodge's career as a pilot; she calls him "King of Pilots."
23. Conley and Campbell, *South Providence*, 8–9; "Glimpses," *Journal*, May 1, 1887, describes Fauvel-Gaurand and provides a detailed view of the pre–Fabre Line south-side waterfront.

Chapter 2

24. *Journal*, May 23, 1911.
25. Ibid., June 18, 1911, July 2, 1911. The stern of the *Germania* swung out of the channel and struck the flats. The encounter came about more as a consequence of the inexperience of the pilot handling the large vessel than lack of sufficient channel width, although the channel was then narrow in this area.
26. Ibid., August 11, 1911.
27. Ibid., July 9, 1911.
28. Ibid., July to August 1911.

29. "Record of Entrances," May to December 1911; *Journal*, May to December 1911.
30. *Journal*, February 27, 1912; "Record of Entrances." The *Sant'Anna* never entered the port of Providence; it was the only Fabre steamer of the period that did not make a Rhode Island visit.
31. *Journal*, September 27 to 28, 1912.
32. Ibid., September 28 to 29, 1912.
33. Ibid., September 27, 1912.
34. Ibid., October 2, 1912.
35. Ibid.
36. "This Is the Time," *Providence*, 387–8; *Journal*, October 2, 1913.
37. *Journal*, October 9 to 10, 1913.
38. Ibid., October 22 to 29, 1913.
39. Ibid., November 7, 1913.
40. Ibid., December 17 to 18, 1913, June 8, 1914. In a curious twist of fate, those Fabre Line ships that berthed at State Pier Number 1 were within one hundred yards of the spot where small transport boats from Newport floated after debarking General Rochambeau's army at its very first encampment on the road to the decisive Revolutionary War battle of Yorktown. The reenactment of that march on its 225th anniversary in 2006 began in June on Dock Conley, just north of the state pier. See "The Road to Independence Passed through Paris; the Road to Yorktown Passed through Providence," in Conley, *People*, 184–95.
41. Carroll, *Rhode Island*, 2:848; "Fabre Line Will Greatly Increase Its Service," *Providence*, 311; Farrelly; O'Neil.
42. *Journal*, February 19, 1914; ibid., April 2, 1914.
43. "Record of Entrances"; U.S. Department of Commerce and Labor, *Annual Report*, Table I (hereafter cited as *Annual Report*). This return trip practice was quite common in Providence and other immigrant landing ports. It is analyzed in Wyman, *Round-Trip*.
44. *Journal*, April 28, 1914.
45. Ibid., June 8, 1914.
46. Ibid., April 20, 1914.
47. Ibid., July 1, 1914; "Send It via Providence," *Providence*, 519.
48. This view is shared by steamship agent Norton W. Nelson; see Nelson.

Chapter 3

49. *Journal*, April to August 1914, passim; "Providence Permanently Linked Up with Marseilles," *Providence*, 302–5.
50. *Record of American*, 788; Bonsor, *North Atlantic*, 386 lists the *Providence* as a ship of 11,990 tons with a length of 512 feet.
51. Potter and Nimitz, *Sea Power*, 455.
52. Maxtone-Graham, *Only Way*, 121.
53. *Journal*, August 16, 1914.
54. Ibid.
55. Ibid., August 23, 1914. The changing of the vessel's name probably took place immediately upon its arrival at New York on August 16, 1914.
56. "Record of Entrances"; *Morton Allen Directory*, 177, 185, 189, 191, 193.
57. *Annual Report*, 1914–1919, Tables I and XXIII.
58. *Journal*, October 11, 1914.
59. Ibid., January 3 and 9, 1915.
60. Ibid., January 22, 1915.
61. Potter and Nimitz, *Sea Power*, 457–8. Excellent accounts of the sinking of the *Lusitania* are Simpson, Lusitania; Bailey and Ryan, Lusitania *Disaster*; and Butler, Lusitania.
62. *Journal*, February 24, 1915; "Record of Entrances."
63. Ibid., March 24 and September 13, 1915.
64. Ibid., September 13, 18, 28, 1915.
65. Ibid., October 9, 21, 1915.
66. Ibid., September 13, 1915.
67. Simpson and Butler show very clearly how the British and their American sympathizers allowed contraband to be hidden by means of false manifests and shipped to Great Britain. It seems reasonable to assume that this might well have been happening aboard Fabre vessels sailing from New York. See the works by Simpson and Butler previously cited. Butler differs slightly from Simpson regarding the amount of armament, while concluding that "the most likely candidate for the second blast [following the strike of the torpedo] is the shipment of fifty-two tons of 3-inch shrapnel shells," 246, 249–51.
68. Potter and Nimitz, *Sea Power*, 458; "Record of Entrances," 1915–16.
69. *Journal*, December 4, 1915.
70. "Record of Entrances," 1916–20.
71. See the papers listing crew members included among Fabre passenger manifests at the United States Custom House in Providence.

72. Potter and Nimitz, *Sea Power*, 458.
73. *Journal*, March 6, 17, 1916.
74. Ibid., May 8, 1916. For an account of operations aboard a German auxiliary cruiser at this time, see Von Niezychowski, *Cruise*.
75. *Journal*, July 11, 1916.
76. Ibid., March 24, 1917; Potter and Nimitz, *Sea Power*, 462.
77. Ibid., April 11, 1918.
78. Ibid., February 8, 1917; *Annual Report*, 1911–1916, Table 1; "Record of Entrances," 1917–19.
79. Potter and Nimitz, *Sea Power*, 460, 466–70.
80. *Journal*, June 21 and July 28, 1919; Bonsor, *North Atlantic*, 384; Sache, "Fabre," http://www.crwflags.com.
81. See Appendix, Table 1.
82. Jones, *American Immigration*, 268–70.
83. Potter and Nimitz, *Sea Power*, 462.
84. *Journal*, February 15 and March 10 and 24, 1917; Appendix, Table 1.

Chapter 4

85. "Rhode Island's Patriot Acts of 1919" in Conley, *People*, 410–15. Higham, *Strangers*, 194–263 is a superb and detailed analysis of this nativistic phenomenon in its national setting. On Rhode Island's immigrant radicalism and native reaction thereto, see Buhle, "Italian-American," *Radical History Review*, 121–51.
86. *Public Laws*, January Session, 1914, chapter 1078, 342–43; *Providence Journal–Bulletin Almanac*, 1914–21.
87. *Public Laws*, January Session, 1919, chapter 1802, 212–15; ibid., chapter 1904, 386–87 (Americanization Act); ibid., chapter 1771, 155–57 (Government Protection Act).
88. Conley, *People*, 413–14; *Journal*, January 1920, passim.
89. Hayman, *Catholicism*, 547; Kellner and Lemons, *Rhode Island*, 76–8; Immigrant Educational Bureau, *Report for the Year Ending, January 1914*, Conley collection.
90. Hayman, *Catholicism*, 724; Carroll, *Rhode Island*, 2:1, 114.
91. *Journal*, January 23, 1919.
92. See Appendix, Table 4.
93. "Record of Entrances," 1919.

94. *Journal,* June 20, 1919; "Fabre Line Will Greatly Increase Its Service," *Providence,* 309–11. The line lost the *Venezia* as a consequence of a fire at sea. The vessel had been chartered to the GGT (French Line) after the armistice. Bonsor, *North Atlantic,* 384.
95. *Journal,* June 20, 1919.
96. "Providence Has an Up-to-the-Minute Dry Dock and Repair Plant," *Providence,* 312–15.
97. *Journal,* June 20, 1919.
98. Ibid.
99. Ibid., July 12, 1919.
100. Ibid., July 26, 1919.
101. Ibid., July 27 to 28, 1919.
102. Ibid., November 13, 1919; "Fabre Line Obtains New Lease," *Providence,* 576.
103. *Journal,* February 26, 1920.
104. Ibid., March 14, 1920.
105. Ibid., June 7, 1920.
106. See Appendix, Table 1.
107. *Annual Report,* 1919–1921; *Journal,* January 23, 1919. See Appendix, Table 3.
108. Twenty Luiz posters and other Fabre Line memorabilia were purchased in 2007 by Patrick T. Conley from Massachusetts collector H.C. Northern Jr. Several of these items have been used to illustrate this volume.
109. "Providence Comes Back to Home Port," *Providence,* 154–6; *Journal,* June 18 to 19, 1920.
110. *Journal,* October 27, 1920.
111. *Annual Report,* 1911–32; "Record of Entrances," 1919–20. See Appendix, Table 4.

Chapter 5

112. Garis, *Immigration Restriction.*
113. Jones, *American Immigration,* 250–2.
114. Garis, *Immigration Restriction,* 115–16.
115. Commager, "Immigration Restriction," in *Documents,* 315–17; Stephenson, *History* contains an analysis of the restrictive legislation from 1917 to 1924 by a learned contemporary.
116. See O'Grady, *Immigrants' Influence.*

117. Higham, "Closing the Gates," chap. 11 in *Strangers*, 300–30; Commager, "Immigration Restriction," in *Documents*, 315–17, 372–73; Jones, "The Consequences of Restriction, 1924–59," chap. 10 in *American Immigration*, 278–307; Hutchinson, "From Regulation to Restriction, 1913–1929," chap. 5 in *Legislative History*, 159–213. A well-researched and detailed local study with statistics is Assis, "Immigration." For an interpretative overview of the impact of the new immigration on Rhode Island, see "The New Immigration and Rhode Island Catholicism," chap. 32 in Conley, *Rhode Island*, 293–8. For the native reaction to it, see "The Persistence of Political Nativism in Rhode Island, 1893–1915: The A.P.A. and Beyond," chap. 49 in Conley, *Rhode Island*, 464–72, which contains a photo of a Ku Klux Klan cross burning in Smithfield in 1927.
118. In 1989, William Conley, a dealer in fine art and antiques, acquired a cache of LeBaron Colt memorabilia and gave it to his brother Patrick. A year later, Patrick Conley donated the collection to Linden Place, Colt's Bristol mansion, which was then in the process of becoming a house museum. He retained one item: Colt's typescript copy of votes taken at the February 28, 1924 meeting of his Senate Immigration Committee, listing the balloting on seven crucial motions made to shape the final act. Conley's donation was given in the presence of a Japanese delegation from Shimoda, Japan, Newport's sister city, as part of the 1990 annual Black Ships Festival. The collection contained several condolences on the death of Colt from Japanese and Chinese officials lamenting the fact that America had lost "a great statesman." For a biographical profile of Colt, see Carroll, *Rhode Island*, 3:5–7.
119. *Journal*, February 8, 1917.
120. Ibid., June 9, 1921. The monthly quota for all of New England in June 1921 allowed for the admission of only thirty Portuguese and three hundred Italian immigrant aliens.
121. Ibid., May 15, 1921.
122. Ibid., May 22, 1921; "Fabre Line Sticks Here," *Providence*, 343.
123. *Journal*, June 9, 1921.
124. This reference is corroborated by Nelson, Farrelly and O'Neil.
125. *Journal*, July 1 and 2, 1921.
126. "Fabre Line Sticks Here," *Providence*, 343.
127. *Journal*, passim; Farrelly. Thomas Farrelly told us of his interesting experience regarding this subject. The steamship companies that carried passengers in excess of the monthly quota were fined by the U.S. Customs Service to the extent of the total amount of money that they were obliged

to refund to their returning passengers; Farrelly would collect the refunded money and send it to Europe, payable at a bank in the immigrant's native land. During this period, many checks remained outstanding for up to two years. To minimize this problem, Farrelly devised a scheme: he went to a local exchange and converted the money that was to be returned into the money of the country of those receiving the refund. On at least one occasion, the bottom fell out of the market in the returnee's country and his returned passage money was valueless, something neither Farrelly nor the customs service had envisioned. Shortly afterward, another procedure was devised to correct this situation.

128. "Record of Entrances," 1921–1922; Appendix, Table 4.
129. *Journal*, July 12, 1923.
130. Ibid., 1923, passim.
131. Ibid., October 11, 1923.
132. Passenger manifests, 1923–34, passim; *Journal*, 1923–34, passim. By the summer of 1923, even the traditional sailing route was slightly varied. The larger vessels of the line sometimes followed a route that began at Marseilles and included calls at Naples, Nice and Algiers, omitting stops at Lisbon and the Azores. This was often the route of the larger steamers of the line that did not begin to call regularly at Providence until the summer of 1927; these vessels, particularly the *Patria* and *Providence*, were on the direct New York run, after a stop at Palermo, Sicily. Some Fabre vessels were sailing on the traditional route that included calls at the Azores. "Providence Permanently Linked Up with Marseilles," *Providence*; "Record of Entrances," 1923–34. The *Roma* arrived at Providence on March 30, 1927—after beginning its passage at Marseilles and calling at Alexandria, Beruit, Jaffe, Constanza, Constantinople, Piraeus and Lisbon—having sailed a total distance of 6,629.5 nautical miles. See *Journal*, March 31, 1927.
133. *Journal*, September 1, 1923.
134. *Annual Report*, 1924; Table 1.
135. Appendix, Table 4.
136. Assis, "Immigration," 8, 17.
137. *Journal*, March 14, 1924.
138. Ibid., June 1, 1924.
139. Ibid., June 30, 1924.
140. Ibid., July 3, 1924.
141. Conley, *People*, 231–2. After Priest's unexpected death, the building reverted to miscellaneous commercial uses and became vacant in

the late 1930s. In 1940, it was acquired by the City Tire Company, which ran a successful business there for six decades before going into receivership. Patrick and Gail Conley acquired the four-story structure in 2002, renamed it Conley's Wharf, spent nearly $7 million on its renovation and secured its listing on the National Register of Historic Places in 2007. In that year, they opened a conference room on the east, or river, side of the fourth floor that became the headquarters of the Rhode Island Publications Society, dba Fabre Line Club. See Rhode Island Historical Preservation and Heritage Commission, (National Register of Historic Places Registration forms,) prepared by Edward Connors, containing a full history of the structure. OMS no. 1024-0018.
142. *Journal,* July 20, 1924. The increased sailings were for the remainder of 1924. The line usually announced its sailings six months in advance.
143. Ibid., September 1, 1924.
144. Ibid., October 15, December 10, 1924.
145. Farrelly; O'Neil.
146. *Journal,* November 15, 1924.
147. Farrelly; O'Neil.
148. *Journal,* November 23, 1924.
149. Ibid., November 4, 1924.
150. *Annual Report,* 1921–25, Tables 1 and 23.
151. *Journal,* July 9, 1925.
152. *Annual Report,* 1921–25, Table 1.
153. Conley and Campbell, *Providence,* 143–4, 248.

Chapter 6

154. "Record of Entrances," 1934.
155. *Journal,* March 15, 1926.
156. Ibid., September 15, 1926.
157. Ibid., December 19, 1926; Bonsor, *North Atlantic,* 386.
158. *Journal,* March 31, 1927; April 1, 1927; "Record of Entrances," 1927.
159. *Journal,* April 1, 2, 5, 11, 1927.
160. Albion, interviewed by Jennings, July 1974.
161. Miller, *Fabre Line.*
162. *Journal,* August 23, 1927; ibid., August 18, 1928.

163. Ibid., June 2, 1927; "Fabre Line Links Providence with the Old World," *Providence*, 114, 116. To cultivate this travel business, the Fabre Line, in conjunction with the Portuguese consul at Providence, awarded six first-class round-trip tickets to Portugal and the Azores to Portuguese and Portuguese Americans living in the United States. The recipients were chosen by means of a contest.
164. "Fabre Line Links Providence," *Providence*. The *Providence Magazine* reported in March 1928 that the Fabre Line had made Providence its "principal landing port," yet the overwhelming amount of cargo came to America through the New York port, leading one to believe that the report was in error.
165. *Journal*, June 13, 1928; *Annual Report*, 1926–34; Appendix, Table 1.
166. *Journal*, May 13, 1928; Appendix, Table 5.
167. *Journal*, September 13, 1928. In December 1934, Ataturk gave Turkish women the vote.
168. Ibid., May 23, 1930.
169. See Appendix, Table 4. The *Asia* recorded twenty-nine arrivals from 1920 through 1929.
170. *Journal*, August 4, 14, 1911; ibid., February 27, 1912; ibid., October 7, 1927; ibid., September 13, 1928; ibid., November 15, 1928. See also Patten, *Rhode Island*, 55–7.
171. *Book of Rhode Island*, 270; *Journal*, 1923–30, passim; "Record of Entrances," 1923–30.
172. Weller, *New Haven*; Loventhal, *Titanic Railroad*.
173. Carroll, *Rhode Island*, 2:850; Conley and Campbell, *Providence*, 179–80.
174. *Journal*, February 26, 1931; Conley and Campbell, *Firefighters*, 82–6.
175. Conley Collection.
176. "Providence Comes Back to Home Port," *Providence*, 156.
177. *Journal*, April 3, 1931; "Record of Entrances ," 1931.
178. "Providence Comes Back to Home Port," *Providence*, 154, 156. The building of the municipal wharf at Providence involved the elimination of Field's Point as a geographical feature by cutting away its sharp projection completely and drawing the harbor line straight. Gone forever were the clambake pavilion and the shore dinners that had been so long associated with the point. The city had constructed a three-thousand-foot quay, dredged the harbor in front and alongside to a depth of thirty-five feet and reclaimed the tidal flats behind part of the wall by washing down a hill with hydraulic equipment. The wall was completed by 1914, and two years later, other work was carried

forward sufficiently to warrant formal dedication. Rail connections with the New Haven were provided by a marine, or marginal, railroad traversing the whole frontage (this was also to be the connection with the projected Southern New England Railroad). Storage tracks on the flats were built for freight handling. Later, the dock was equipped with freight houses, traveling cranes and other modern machinery. See Carroll, *Rhode Island*, 2:848; Conley and Campbell, *Providence*, 149–52; Cady, *Civic*.

179. *Journal*, May 10, 1931.
180. Ibid., May 31, 1931.
181. Farrelly; O'Neil; Carroll, *Rhode Island*, 2:1,157.
182. *Journal*, May 31, 1931; "Record of Entrances ," 1931–34.
183. *Journal*, September 18, 1934; "SS *Rochambeau*."
184. *Journal*, June 27, 1934
185. Ibid., July 5, 1934; "SS *Rochambeau*."
186. *Journal*, November 6, 1934.
187. Bonsor, *North Atlantic*, 384; Farrelly; O'Neil; Nelson.
188. See Appendix, Table 5; "Fabre Line," Ships List, http.//www.theshipslist.com/ship/descriptions.
189. Appendix, Table 5.
190. For the visits of the *Patria* to Providence, see Appendix, Table 4; for this ship's ultimate fate, see "SS *Patria* (1913)."
191. Bonsor, *North Atlantic*, 385; Gibbs, *Passenger Liners*, 341; Sache, "Fabre," http://www.crwflags.com.
192. *Journal*, December 11, 1958.

Chapter 7

193. Farrelly; O'Neil; *Journal*, 1911–34, passim.
194. *Annual Report*, 1912–14; Appendix, Table 1.
195. *Annual Report*, 1915–16; Appendix, Table 1; "Record of Entrances," 1917–19.
196. *Annual Report*, 1921–24; Appendix, Table 1.
197. *Annual Report*, 1924–25; Appendix, Table 1.
198. Passenger manifests, 1923–24.
199. Ibid., 1921–24. The passenger manifests for the months immediately preceding November 1923 contain names of individuals apparently from

Middle Eastern countries, although no Middle Eastern ports of origin are listed on these manifests.
200. This observation is made in Assis, "Immigration," a meticulously researched analysis of immigration to Rhode Island during the first three decades of the twentieth century. This analysis, prepared in a 1973 master's-level seminar at Providence College under the direction of Patrick T. Conley, examined the years for which detailed records of immigration were maintained by the U.S. Immigration and Naturalization Service. This work by Dr. Assis remains the best study of this process and merits publication.
201. Farrelly; O'Neil; *Journal*, 1920–29, passim.
202. *Annual Report*, 1920–29; Appendix, Table 1.
203. *Annual Report*, 1911–32; Appendix, Table 1.
204. *Annual Report*, 1915–21; Appendix, Table 2; *Journal*, 1911–21, passim; Assis, "Immigration," 59.
205. *Journal*, 1911–34, passim; Appendix, Table 2.
206. *Annual Report*, 1911–32; Appendix, Table 2.
207. On Woonsocket's diversity, see Wessel, *Ethnic Survey*. From 1911 to 1915, Wessel held the position of director of the Immigrant Educational Bureau in Providence.
208. U.S. Immigration, *Records*.
209. Appendix, Table 3.
210. Assis, "Immigration," passim; Conley, *Album*, 161–2.
211. *Annual Report*, 1911–20; Appendix, Table 3; Passenger manifests, 1911–24, passim; "Record of Entrances," 1911–24; *Journal*, 1911–24, passim.
212. "Record of Entrances," 1911–34; *Journal*, 1911–34, passim.
213. Passenger manifests, 1911–34; Bonsor, *North Atlantic*, 384.
214. *Journal*, 1911–34, passim; O'Neil.
215. *Journal*, October 2, 1923.
216. Ibid., June 17, 1911.
217. Ibid., September 28, 1912; O'Neil.
218. Baggage manifests, 1922–34.
219. *Journal*, June 9, 1914.
220. Ibid., July 2, 1922.
221. Ibid., July 2, 1911.
222. "When the Big Ships Come into This Port," *Providence*, 583.
223. *Journal*, June 18, 1911; ibid., August 1, 1911.
224. Hayman, *Catholicism*, 499–501, 546–7; Cullen, *Catholic Church*, which contains brief profiles of every ethnic parish, every religious order

operating in the Diocese of Providence and the various Catholic societies; Farrelly; O'Neil. See also McActee, "National Parish."
225. Hayman, *Catholicism*, 546–7.
226. Ibid., 499–501. This well-researched volume spans the productive episcopacy of Bishop Harkins (1886–1921). See also "Bishop Matthew Harkins: A Study in Character" and "Matthew Harkins: The Bishop of the Poor" chapts. 38 and 39 in Conley, *Rhode Island*.
227. O'Neil; Foster, Horvitz and Cohen, *Jews*, 28.
228. Conley and Campbell, *South Providence*, 9, 72–3, 95–6, 102–03.
229. "When the Big Ships Come," *Providence*, 583.
230. *Journal*, November 8, 1928.
231. O'Neil.
232. Ibid.
233. O'Neil; Farrelly; *Journal*, 1911–34, passim.
234. Passenger manifest of the *Sinaia*, April 18, 1931.
235. *Journal*, July 2, 1932.
236. O'Neil. An excellent description of passenger accommodations to America on transatlantic steamers of this era is Taylor, *Distant Magnet*, chap. 8.
237. *Journal*, June 27, 1934.
238. O'Neil.
239. *Journal*, December 11, 1958.
240. *Annual Report*, 1920–30; Appendix, Table 1; Farrelly; O'Neil.
241. Thernstom, *Harvard Encyclopedia* contains information and insightful essays written by specialists on every American ethnic group. For accounts of Rhode Island ethnic communities, including all of those associated with the Fabre Line, see Beade, *Wealth of Nations*; Patrick T. Conley, ed., Rhode Island Ethnic Heritage Pamphlet Series, 14 vols. (Providence: Rhode Island Heritage Commission and Rhode Island Publications Society, 1985–95); "Ethnic Profiling: Brief Surveys of Rhode Island's Major Immigrant Communities," chap. 11 in Conley, *People*, 70–127; and Bouvier and Corless, *Ethnic Profile*.
242. Pesaturo, *Italo-Americans*; Boyden, "Brief History," *Providence News*; Carroll, *Rhode Island*, 2:1,154–57. These are good contemporary accounts. Muratore, *Italian-Americans* are fully illustrated works by the state's leading historian of the Rhode Island Italian American community. Using a similar format is Fuoco, *Federal Hill*. More scholarly accounts include Bardaglio, "Italian Immigrants," *Rhode Island History*, 47–57; Smith, *Family Connections*; Santoro, *Italians in Rhode Island*; Colangelo, "Italians"; Earnshaw, "Italian Immigration"; Fioravante,

"Italian Community"; Carroll, *Voices*; "The Rise of Rhode Island's Italian American Community, 1880–1932," chap. 33 in Conley, *Rhode Island*, 299–306; and Watkinson, "Italian Immigrant." On Italian immigration figures, see Assis, "Immigration," passim.

243. On the local Portuguese community, see Cunha, Pacheco and Wolfson, *Portuguese*; Ferst, "Immigration"; Ussach, "Portuguese"; and Handler, "Azoreans," *Hidden Minorities*. The story of the Cape Verdeans, who were then Portuguese nationals, can be found in Coli and Lobban, *Cape Verdeans*; Halter, "Cape Verdean-American Immigration"; and Meintel, "Cape Verdean," *Hidden Minorities*.

244. Assis, "Immigration," 44, 120.

245. Ibid., 36–7, 49, 76. Numerous essays on various aspects of local Jewish life can be found in the *Rhode Island Jewish Historical Notes*, the journal of the Rhode Island Jewish Historical Association. Useful general accounts are Smith, *Family Connections*; Foster, *Jews*; Foster, Horvitz and Cohen, *Jews*; Goldstein, *Greater Providence*; and Goodwin and Smith, *Jews*.

246. Assis, "Immigration," 49, 76, 118, 120.

247. Mowatt, *Ukrainians*; "The Ukrainians of Rhode Island: The Founding and the Fragmentation of an Ethnic Community, 1903–1938," chap. 34 in Conley, *Rhode Island*, 307–14.

248. Kyriakou and Georas, *Greek People*; Anttio, "Greek Community."

249. Doumato, *Arabic-Speaking People*; Smith, "Arabic Speaking Communities," in *Hidden Minorities*; "Rhode Island's Christian Arabs: The Origins of the Syrian-Lebanese Community," in chap. 35 *Rhode Island*, 315–19.

250. Gelenian, *Armenians*.

251. On the availability of jobs as a magnet for immigrants to Rhode Island, see Mayer and Goldstein, *Migration*.

Chapter 8

252. U.S. Army Corps of Engineers, *United States Water-Bourne Foreign Commerce*, s.v. "Providence"; "Records of Entrances," 1,911–34.

253. *Journal*, October 29, 1912.

254. Ibid., November 30, 1913.

255. Ibid., December 18, 1913.

256. Ibid., July 15, 1914.

257. Ibid., October 29, 1929.
258. During the 1920s, the duty on Madeira lace was 90 percent of its value, the highest paid on any foreign commodity. Often, attempts were made to smuggle this item; see *Journal*, March 15, 1922. The yams from Portugal were barred by the U.S. Department of Agriculture if they had any trace of soil on them. Those Portuguese who carried yams as part of their belongings washed them before customs officials inspected them; see O'Neil.
259. Farrelly; O'Neil.
260. *Journal*, February 27, 1917.
261. U.S. Army Corps of Engineers, *United States Water-Bourne Foreign Commerce*, 1,922–34.
262. Carroll, *Rhode Island*, 2:848–49, 926; "Record of Entrances," 1911–34; U.S. Army Corps of Engineers, *United States Water-Bourne Foreign Commerce*, 1,922–34.
263. *Journal*, February 15, 1917.

BIBLIOGRAPHY

Primary Sources
Public Documents

The Public Laws of the State of Rhode Island and Providence Plantations. Providence, RI: E.L. Freeman Company and Oxford Press, 1911–34.

U.S. Army Corps of Engineers. *United States Water-Borne Foreign Commerce*. Washington, D.C.: Government Printing Office, 1911–34.

U.S. Department of Commerce and Labor. *Annual Report of the Commissioner General of Immigration for the Fiscal Year*. Washington, D.C.: Government Printing Office, 1905–12.

U.S. Department of Labor. *Annual Report of the Commissioner General of Immigration for the Fiscal Year*. Washington, D.C.: Government Printing Office, 1913–32.

———. Series XI. *Inventory of Federal Archives in the States: No. 38, Rhode Island*. Providence, RI: National Archives Project, 1938. An inventory of the records of the Rhode Island immigration and naturalization service (naturalization by RI Superior Courts).

U.S. Immigration and Naturalization Service. *Records of the Immigration and Naturalization Service, 1891–1957, Record Group 85, Providence, Rhode Island*. Book indexes to Providence passenger lists, 1911–1934, T792, 15 rolls. National Archives.

BIBLIOGRAPHY

U.S. Shipping Board. *Report on the Volume of Water-Borne Foreign Commerce of the United States by Ports of Origin and Destination.* Washington, D.C.: Government Printing Office, 1922–35.

Providence Custom House Records

Baggage manifests of Fabre vessels entering the port of Providence, 1911–34.
Passenger manifests of Fabre vessels entering the port of Providence, 1911–34.
"Record of Entrances and Clearances of Vessels Engaged in Foreign Trade, Port of Providence." 3 vols. 1911–34.

Newspapers and Articles Appearing in Newspapers

Boyden, Ben. "A Brief History of Rhode Island Italians, 1880–1924." *Providence News*, August 27–29, September 2–5, 1924.
Providence Journal. "Glimpses of the Early History of South Providence." May 1, 1887.
———. 1910–34.
Providence Journal–Bulletin Almanac. 1911–34.

Articles Appearing in Magazines

"Fabre Line Brings Nearly Twelve Thousand Aliens to Providence." *Providence Magazine: The Board of Trade Journal* 25 (August 1913): 303.
"Fabre Line Links Providence with the Old World." *Providence Magazine: The Board of Trade Journal* 39 (March 1928): 114–16.
"Fabre Line Obtains New Lease." *Providence Magazine: The Board of Trade Journal* 31 (November 1919): 576.
"Fabre Line Sticks Here." *Providence Magazine: The Board of Trade Journal* 33 (July 1921): 343.
"Fabre Line Will Greatly Increase Its Service." *Providence Magazine: The Board of Trade Journal* 31 (July 1919): 309–11.
"Once More in Providence Harbor." *Providence Magazine: The Board of Trade Journal* 31 (April 1919): 169–70.
"Providence Comes Back to Home Port." *Providence Magazine: The Board of Trade Journal* 42 (May 1931): 154–56.

Bibliography

"Providence Has Up-to-the-Minute Dry Dock and Repair Plant." *Providence Magazine: The Board of Trade Journal* 31 (July 1919): 312–15.

"Providence Permanently Linked Up with Marseilles." *Providence Magazine: The Board of Trade Journal* 35 (June 1923): 302–5.

"Send It Via Providence." *Providence Magazine: The Board of Trade Journal* 25 (July 1914): 519.

"This Is the Time of a Thorough Waking-Up." *Providence Magazine: The Board of Trade Journal* 25 (October 1913): 387–88.

"When the Big Ships Come into This Port." *Providence Magazine: The Board of Trade Journal* 35 (November 1923): 585.

Books And Other Printed Material

The Book of Rhode Island. Providence: Rhode Island Conference of Business Associations, 1930.

Commager, Henry Steele, ed. "Immigration Restriction: The Laws of 1917 and 1921" and "The Immigration Act of 1924," in *Documents of American History*. 6th ed. New York: Appleton-Century-Crofts, 1958; quoted from U.S. Department of Labor. *Annual Report of the Commissioner General of Immigration*. Washington, D.C.: Government Printing Office, 1923–4.

Kirk, William, ed. *A Modern City: Providence, Rhode Island, and Its Activities*. Chicago: University of Chicago Press, 1909.

Miller, Warren Hastings. *The Fabre Line Mediterranean Cruises: What to See and Do Ashore*. Marseilles, France: Maurin and Pages, 1925.

Morton Allen Directory of European Passenger Steamship Arrivals for the Years 1890 to 1930 to the Port of New York. New York: Immigrant Information Bureau, 1931.

Patten, David. *Rhode Island Story: Recollections of 35 Years on the Staff of the* Providence Journal *and the* Evening Bulletin. Providence, RI: Providence Journal Company, 1954.

Record of American and Foreign Shipping. New York: American Bureau of Shipping, 1911–34.

Von Niezychowski, Count Alfred. *The Cruise of the* Kronprinz Wilhelm. Garden City, NY: Doubleday, Doran & Company, 1929.

Bibliography

Interviews

Albion, Robert G., Director, Munson Institute, Mystic Seaport. Interview by William Jennings, July 1974.

Carroll, Barbara R., ed. *Voices of Rhode Island's Italian-Americans*. North Providence, RI: Hopkins Press, 2012.

Connelly, Thomas L., Director of Inspection and Controls and Supervisory Inspector of Customs, Providence Custom House. Interview by William Jennings, July 11, 1974.

Farrelly, Thomas F., former employee of the U.S. Customs Service at Providence and New York (deputy collector at New York). Interview by William Jennings, July 17, 1974.

———. Interview by Patrick T. Conley and Matthew J. Smith, August 31, 1972. Transcript at Providence College Archives.

Mahoney, John, clerk at Municipal Pier, Providence. Interview by William Jennings, July 19, 1974.

Nelson, Norton W., president and owner of Goff & Page, Inc., former Providence agents of the Fabre Line. Interview by William Jennings, July 10, 1974.

O'Neil, James F., former employee of the U.S. Customs Service at Providence (deputy collector at Providence). Interviews by William Jennings, July 17 and 19, 1974.

Collection

Patrick T. Conley. Private collection of Fabre Line memorabilia.

Secondary Sources

Books

Bailey, Thomas A., and Paul B. Ryan. *The* Lusitania *Disaster: An Episode in Modern Warfare and Diplomacy*. New York: Simon and Schuster, 1975.

Beade, Lisa Roseman. *The Wealth of Nations: A Peoples' History of Rhode Island*. Montgomery, AL: Community Communication, 1999.

Bodnar, John. *The Transplanted: A History of Immigrants in Urban America*. Bloomington: University of Indiana Press, 1985.

Bois, Paul. *Armements marseillais—Compagnies de navigation et navires à vapeur, 1831–1988*. Marseilles, France: Chamber of Commerce and Industry, 1988.

Bibliography

Bonsor, N.R.P. *North Atlantic Seaway*. Prescot, Lancashire, England: Stephenson & Sons, 1955.

Bouvier, Leon F., and Inge B. Corless. *An Ethnic Profile of the State of Rhode Island*. Kingston: University of Rhode Island, 1968.

Brye, David L., ed. *European Immigration and Ethnicity in the United States and Canada: A Historical Bibliography*. Santa Barbara, CA: Clio Press, Inc., 1983.

Butler, Daniel Allen. *The Lusitania: The Life, Loss, and Legacy of an Ocean Legend*. Mechanicsburg, PA: Stackpole Books, 2000.

Cady, John Hutchins. *The Civic and Architectural Development of Providence, 1636–1950*. Providence, RI: Book Shop, 1957.

Carroll, Charles. *Rhode Island: Three Centuries of Democracy*. 4 vols. New York: Lewis Historical Publishing Company, 1932.

Climent, James, ed. *Encyclopedia of Immigration*. 4 vols. Armonk, NY: Sharpe Reference, 2001.

Coli, Waltraud Berger, and Richard A. Lobban. *The Cape Verdians in Rhode Island: A Brief History*. Rhode Island Ethnic Heritage Pamphlet Series. Providence: Rhode Island Heritage Commission and Rhode Island Publications Society, 1985.

Columbia Lippincott Gazetteer of the World. New York: Columbia University Press, 1952.

Conley, Patrick T. *An Album of Rhode Island History, 1636–1986*. Norfolk, VA: Donning Company, 1986.

———. *People, Places, Laws and Lore of the Ocean State*. Providence: Rhode Island Publications Society, 2012.

———. *Rhode Island in Rhetoric and Reflection*. Providence: Rhode Island Publications Society, 2002.

Conley, Patrick T., and Paul R. Campbell. *Firefighters and Fires in Providence: A Pictorial History of the Providence Fire Department, 1754–2001*. Providence: Rhode Island Publications Society, 2002.

———. *Providence: A Pictorial History*. Norfolk, VA: Donning Company, 1982.

———. *South Providence*. Charleston, SC: Arcadia Publishers, 2006.

Cullen, Thomas F. *The Catholic Church in Rhode Island*. Providence, RI: Franciscan Missionaries of Mary, 1936.

Cunha, M. Rachel, Susan A. Pacheco and Beth Pereira Wolfson. *The Portuguese in Rhode Island: A History*. Rhode Island Ethnic Heritage Pamphlet Series. Providence: Rhode Island Heritage Commission and Rhode Island Publications Society, 1985.

Doumato, Eleanor A. *The Arabic-Speaking People in Rhode Island: A Centenary Celebration*. Rhode Island Ethnic Heritage Pamphlet Series. Providence:

Bibliography

Rhode Island Heritage Commission and Rhode Island Publications Society, 1986.

Foster, Geraldine S. *The Jews in Rhode Island: A Brief History*. Rhode Island Ethnic Heritage Pamphlet Series. Providence: Rhode Island Heritage Commission and Rhode Island Publications Society, 1985.

Foster, Geraldine S., Eleanor F. Horvitz and Judith Weiss Cohen. *Jews of Rhode Island, 1658-1958*. Charleston, SC: Arcadia Publishers, 1998.

Fuoco, Joe. *Federal Hill*. Charleston, SC: Arcadia Publishers, 1996.

Garis, Roy L. *Immigration Restriction: A Study of the Opposition to and Regulation of Immigration into the United States*. New York: Macmillan Company, 1927.

Geake, Robert A. *A History of the Providence River*. Charleston, SC: The History Press, 2012.

Gelenian, Ara Arthur. *The Armenians in Rhode Island: Ancient Roots to Present Experiences*. Rhode Island Ethnic Heritage Pamphlet Series. Providence: Rhode Island Heritage Commission and Rhode Island Publications Society, 1985.

Gibbs, Commander C.R. Vernon. *Passenger Liners of the Western Ocean: A Record of the North Atlantic Steam and Motor Passenger Vessels from 1838 to the Present Day*. 2nd rev. ed. London: Staples Press, 1957.

Goldstein, Sidney. *The Greater Providence Jewish Community: A Population Survey*. Providence, RI: General Jewish Committee of Providence, 1964.

Goodwin, George M., and Ellen Smith, eds. *The Jews of Rhode Island*. Waltham, MA: Brandeis University Press, 2004.

Hayman, Robert W. *Catholicism in Rhode Island and the Diocese of Providence, 1886-1921*. Providence, RI: Diocese of Providence, 1995.

Heppner, Frank. *Railroads of Rhode Island*. Charleston, SC: The History Press, 2012.

Higham, John. *Strangers in the Land: Patterns of American Nativism, 1860-1925*. New Brunswick, NJ: Rutgers University Press, 1988.

Hoehling, A.A., and Mary Hoehling. *The Last Voyage of the* Lusitania. New York: Henry Holt & Company, 1956.

Hutchinson, E.P. *Legislative History of American Immigration Policy, 1798-1965*. Philadelphia: University of Pennsylvania Press, 1981.

Jones, Maldwyn Allen. *American Immigration*. Chicago: University of Chicago Press, 1970.

Karr, Ronald Dale. *The Rail Lines of Southern New England*. Pepperell, MA: Branch Line Press, 1995.

Kellner, George H., and J. Stanley Lemons. *Rhode Island: The Independent State*. Woodland Hills, CA: Windsor Publications, 1982.

Bibliography

Kyriakou, Reverend Stephen, and Venetia B. Georas. *The Greek People in Rhode Island: Three Communities, One Ethos, 1893–1993*. Rhode Island Ethnic Heritage Pamphlet Series. Providence: Rhode Island Heritage Commission and Rhode Island Publications Society, 1994.

Lowenthal, Larry. *Titanic Railroad: The Southern New England; The Story of New England's Last Great Railroad War*. Brimfield, MA: Marker Press, 1998.

Maxtone-Graham, John. *The Only Way to Cross*. New York: Macmillian Company, 1972.

Mayer, Kurt B., and Sidney Goldstein. *Migration and Economic Development in Rhode Island*. Providence, RI: Brown University Press, 1958.

McAdam, Roger Williams. *The Old Fall River Line*. New York: Stephen Day Press, 1955.

Mowatt, Right Reverend John J., ed. *The Ukrainians in Rhode Island: Faith and Determination*. Rhode Island Ethnic Heritage Pamphlet Series. Providence: Rhode Island Heritage Commission and Rhode Island Publications Society, 1988.

Muratore, Joseph R. *Italian Americans in Rhode Island*. 2 vols. Charleston, SC: Arcadia Publishing, 1997 and 2000.

Nugent, Walter. *Crossings: The Great Transatlantic Migrations, 1870–1914*. Bloomington: Indiana University Press, 1992.

O'Grady, Joseph P., ed. *The Immigrants' Influence on Wilson's Peace Policies*. Lexington: University of Kentury Press, 1967.

Pesaturo, Ubaldo. *Italo-Americans of Rhode Island*. Rev. ed. Providence, RI: Visitor Printing Co., 1940.

Potter, E.B., and Chester W. Nimitz. *Sea Power: A Naval History*. Englewood Cliffs, NJ: Prentice-Hall, 1960.

Rose, Mary H. "Maizie". *Block Island Scrapbook*. New York: Pagent Press, 1957.

Santoro, Carmela E. *The Italians in Rhode Island: The Age of Exploration to the Present, 1524–1989*. Rhode Island Ethnic Heritage Pamphlet Series. Providence: Rhode Island Heritage Commission and Rhode Island Publications Society, 1990.

Simpson, Colin. *The* Lusitania*: The Life, Loss, and Legacy of an Ocean Legend*. Boston: Little, Brown & Company, 1972.

Smith, Eugene W. *Trans-Atlantic Passenger Ships Past and Present*. Boston: George H. Dean Company, 1947.

Smith, Judith E. *Family Connections: A History of Italian and Jewish Immigrant Lives in Providence, Rhode Island, 1900–1940*. Albany: State University of New York Press, 1985.

Stephenson, George M. *A History of American Immigration, 1820–1924*. Boston: Ginn & Company, 1926.

Sterne, Evelyn Savidge. *Ballots & Bibles: Ethnic Politics and the Catholic Church in Providence*. Ithaca, NY: Cornell University Press, 2004.
Taylor, Philip. *The Distant Magnet: European Emigration to the U.S.A.* London: Eyre & Spottiswoode, 1971.
Taylor, William Leonard. *A Productive Monopoly: The Effect of Railroad Control on New England Costal Steamship Lines, 1870–1916*. Providence, RI: Brown University Press, 1970.
Thernstrom, Stephan, ed. *Harvard Encyclopedia of American Ethnic Groups*. Cambridge, MA: Harvard University Press, 1980.
Weigold, Marilyn E. *The American Mediterranean: An Environmental, Economic & Social History of Long Island Sound*. Port Washington, NY: Kennikat Press, 1974.
Weller, John L. *The New Haven Railroad: Its Rise and Fall*. New York: Hastings House, 1969.
Wessel, Bessie Bloom. *An Ethnic Survey of Woonsocket, Rhode Island*. Chicago: University of Chicago Press, 1931.
Wyman, Mark. *Round-Trip to America: The Immigrants Return to Europe, 1880–1930*. Ithaca, NY: Cornell University Press, 1993.

Articles

Bardaglio, Peter. "Italian Immigrants and the Catholic Church in Providence, 1890–1930." *Rhode Island History* 34 (May 1975): 47–57.
Breed, Donald D. "Goff & Page: 100 Years in Port of Providence." *Providence Journal*, July 2, 1972: Section G8.
Buhle, Paul. "Italian-American Radicals and Labor in Rhode Island, 1905–1930." *Radical History Review* 17 (1978): 121–51.
Byrnes, Garrett D. "Providence, Passenger Port." *Rhode Island*, September 24, 1961: 14–7.
Conley, Patrick T. "Providence and the Fabre Line." *Steamboat Bill: The Journal of the Steamship Historical Society of America*, no. 270 (Summer 2009): 21–27.
"Fabre Line." The Ships List. http://www.theshipslist.com/ships/lines/fabre.html (accessed 2013).
Handler, Mark J. "Azoreans in America: Migration and Change Reconsidered" in *Hidden Minorities: The Persistence of Ethnicity in American Life*. Edited by Joan Rollins. Washington, D.C.: University Press of America, 1981.
Meintel, Deidre. "Cape Verdean Americans" in *Hidden Minorities: The Persistence of Ethnicity in American Life*. Edited by Joan Rollins. Washington, D.C.: University Press of America, 1981.

Bibliography

Patten, David. "The Railroad that Perished at Sea." *Rhode Island Yearbook*, 1969: H 140–5.

Providence Journal. "Coming to America." A nine-part series on Rhode Island immigration by various journalists, published between July 6, 1986, and November 23, 1986.

Sache, Ivan. "Fabre (Shipping Company, France)." http://www.crwflags.com (accessed 2013).

Smith, Marlene Khoury. "The Arabic-Speaking Communities in Rhode Island: A Survey of the Syrian and Lebanese Communities" in *Hidden Minorities: The Persistence of Ethnicity in American Life.* Edited by Joan Rollins. Washington, D.C., University Press of America, 1981.

Stephenson, George M. "Immigration Act of 1924," "Immigration" and "Italian Immigration." *Dictionary of American History.* New York: Charles Scribner's Sons, 1940.

"SS *Patria* (1913)." https://en.wickipedia.org/wiki/SSPatria1988 (accessed 2013).

"SS *Rochambeau*." http://en.wikipedia.org/wiki/SSRochambeau (accessed 2013).

Tanner, Mary C. "European Invasion." *Rhode Island Yearbook*, 1968: H 122–5.

Unpublished Materials

Anttio, George F. "The Greek Community of Rhode Island." Master's seminar paper, Providence College, 1974.

Assis, E. James. "Immigration to Rhode Island, 1898 to 1932: The Major Trends." Master's seminar paper, Providence College, 1973.

Colangelo, John P. "Italians in Providence, 1900–1930." Honors thesis, Brown University, 1974.

Connolly, Christina H. "The Rise and Fall of the Fabre Line, 1911–1934." Senior thesis, Brown University, 1997.

Earnshaw, Donlad J. "Italian Immigration to Rhode Island to 1914." Master's seminar paper, Providence College, 1973.

Ferst, Susan Terry. "The Immigration and the Settlement of the Portuguese in Providence, 1890 to 1924." Master's thesis, Brown University, 1972.

Fioravanti, Joseph. "The Italian Community in Rhode Island, 1914–1941." Master's seminar paper, Providence College, 1973.

Halter, Marilyn B. "Cape Verdean-American Immigration and Patterns of Settlement, 1860–1940." Doctoral dissertation, Boston University, 1986.

McAtee, William J. "The National Parish in Rhode Island." Master's seminar paper, Providence College, 1973.

Smith, Marlene Khoury. "A Profile of the Syrian and Lebanese Communities of Rhode Island." Master's seminar paper, Providence College, 1973.

BIBLIOGRAPHY

Ussach, Betty I. "The Portuguese in Rhode Island." Master's seminar paper, Providence College, 1973.

Watkinson, Margaret M. "The Italian Immigrant and the Roman Catholic Church in Rhode Island, 1880–1924." Master's seminar paper, Providence College, 1976.

INDEX

A

accidents 44, 125, 147
accommodations 19, 28, 32, 34, 35, 36, 37, 40, 41, 43, 57, 74, 97, 100, 107, 108, 120, 125, 133
Adriatic Sea 55, 75, 79
Aegean Sea 75, 77, 94
Albion, Dr. Robert G. 97
Alesia 44, 68, 100, 125
Alexandria 85, 97, 195
Algiers 85, 97, 195
American Citizenship Campaign 68
American Cruise Line 153
Americanization classes 65, 66
American Red Cross 89, 131
An Act to Promote Americanization 64, 65
Annunciation Greek Orthodox Church 140
Aquidneck Island 122
Arabia 100, 144

Archdiocese of Boston 133
Armenian Euphrates Evangelical Protestant Church 141
Armenians 85, 95, 130, 141
Arrow 152
Asia 18, 44, 59, 68, 75, 94, 95, 99, 100
Assumption Greek Orthodox Church 140
Atlantic Ocean 16, 17, 40, 49–51, 53, 54, 56, 69, 78, 82, 84, 85, 87, 88, 94, 99, 103, 107–109, 113, 114, 120, 124, 134, 136, 139, 141, 143, 151–153
Austria 47, 51, 55, 59, 64, 75, 81, 100
Azores 25, 29, 34, 51–54, 59, 68, 70–72, 74, 85, 97, 110, 113, 123, 124, 133, 134, 136–138, 147, 148, 152, 189, 195, 197

INDEX

B

baggage 35, 100, 108, 126, 127, 128
Barcelona 54, 139
Barrington 119
Beirut 97, 141
Bernhard Ingelsson 115
Binning, Helen I. 132
"birds of passage" 87, 135
Black Sea 77, 85, 89, 102, 119, 124, 125, 131, 140, 152
Blackstone Valley 122, 123
Block Island 29, 103, 104
Bloom, Bessie E. 35, 67
Bolsheviks 63, 67
Boston 16, 25, 37, 69, 95, 102, 106, 126, 127, 132, 133, 139, 148
Braga 59, 68, 75, 94, 100
"Brava packets" 108–110, 120, 137
Brazil (Brazilian) 59, 75, 101
Bristol 34, 82, 119, 138, 194
Britannia 18, 43, 52, 54, 68, 69, 72, 74, 89, 91, 99, 121, 124
British-India Steam Navigation Company 115
brochure 96, 102
Brooklyn 20, 24, 89, 90
Brown University 27, 32, 67
Bulgarians 140
Bureau of Immigration (U.S.) 42, 123, 135

C

Cady, John Hutchins 60
California 119, 122, 123, 132, 137
Calve, Emma 52, 53
Canada 14, 23, 27, 89, 99, 105, 140, 150, 151
Canada (ship) 34, 49, 54, 68, 70, 85, 90, 99, 124, 125
Canadian Pacific Railroad 23, 100
Cape Cod 15, 16, 25, 71, 110, 119, 122, 130, 137
Cape Verde 72, 104, 108, 109, 110, 120, 137, 147
Catholic Church 67, 128, 130, 138, 140
Central Falls 140, 141
channel 16, 25, 29, 34, 36, 37, 70, 71, 90, 106
Chapin, Dr. Charles V. 32
cholera 32, 34
churches 67, 68, 130, 140
Clarke, Prescott O. 67
Coldwell, Joseph M. 67
Colonial Line 113, 152
Colt, LeBaron Bradford 82
Columbus Exchange Bank 71, 132
Commonwealth Pier (Boston) 102, 106
Communists 63, 139
Conant, Mr. and Mrs. Samuel M. 49, 53
Conley's Wharf 38, 149, 196
Connecticut 122, 144
Constantinople 97
Constanza 85, 97, 140
"contagious building" 127
convoys 54, 59, 60
Coolidge, President Calvin 80, 105
Cousinery, Dr. Albert 68–70
Cranston 119
Cumberland Farms 150
customs duty 90, 126, 134, 145, 147, 202

Index

D

DeBarros, Reverend M.C. 128
Deschelles, Pierre 57, 87
detainees 32, 41, 95, 127
Diaz, Generalissimo Armando Vittorio 64
diversity 123, 153
Dock Conley 153
Dodge, Tal 29, 72, 103, 104
dredging 16, 25, 27, 31, 32, 34, 60, 70
Drooge, J.A. 35, 36

E

East Bay 24, 119, 122
East Providence 16, 24, 60, 128, 138, 148
economic opportunity 87, 105, 140, 141
Egypt 85
1890 census 81, 82
Ellis Island 20, 88, 136, 153
Emergency Quota Act of 1921 71, 77, 79, 80, 82–84, 119, 121, 124, 146
Ernestina 137
exports 23, 55, 70, 143, 146, 147, 153

F

Fabre, Cyprien 17, 18, 110, 115
Fabre, L. Cyprien 84
Fabre Line Club 154
Fall River 24, 119, 122, 130, 137, 139
Fall River Line 152

farms 27, 119, 135
Farrelly, Thomas 90, 108, 110, 147
Federal Hill 24, 119, 135, 140, 145
Field's Point 15, 16, 56, 60, 106, 197
fire 15, 39, 40, 44, 54, 59, 68, 75, 100, 105, 105–108, 148
Fitzsimmons, Frank E. 58
Fletcher, Mayor Henry 26
Foch, Marshal Ferdinand 64
foodstuffs 24, 106, 143, 144, 146, 148, 151
Foran Act 78
Fox Point 15, 24, 27, 29, 35–37, 60, 71, 119, 122, 126, 128, 137, 138, 144
France 17, 27, 29, 43, 51, 57, 73, 74, 87, 113, 114, 121, 144
fraudulent papers 94
French Line 17, 18, 40, 110, 112

G

Gainer, Mayor Joseph 42, 56, 67
Gallagher, William 105
Garis, Ray L. 78, 79
Gaurand, J.B.G. Fauvel 29
general assembly 23, 45, 64, 82, 106
genocide 141
Germania 19, 31, 34, 43, 50–52, 68, 103
Germany 19, 43, 49, 52, 53, 55, 56, 59, 61, 73, 75, 78, 110, 114, 125
Gibraltar 50, 54, 139
Glasgow 100, 110, 113
Goff, Henry 44
Goff & Page 45, 54, 71, 83, 84, 133
Grand Trunk Railroad 13, 21, 23, 24, 55, 150, 151

Index

Great Crash 105
Great Depression 75, 89, 91, 93, 99, 104, 113, 115, 117, 119, 146, 152
Greece 79, 94, 95, 124, 134, 140, 144
Greek immigration 63, 85, 95, 130, 140
Guez, Gabriel 36, 37
Guilherme M. Luiz and Company 72, 110
Gulf of Mexico 60, 115, 148
Guny, Elizabeth 130, 131

H

Haifa 114, 115, 141
Halifax 88, 89, 140
Hamburg 19, 125
Hamlin, Theophilus 100
Harbor Junction 24, 40, 150
harbormaster 105–107
Harding, President Warren 83
Harkins, Bishop Matthew 128, 130, 138
Harris Lumber Company 148
Hays, Charles M. 21, 23
Hebrew Aid Society 130, 131
Holmes, George 69, 70
hospital ship 54, 59, 69, 110, 113
hurricane of 1938 148, 152
Husbands, William H. 95
hyphenated Americanism 63–65

I

Illinois 122
Immigrant Educational Bureau 35, 67
immigration restriction 78–80, 88
Imperial Warehouse Company 89, 149
imports 23, 24, 55, 69, 78, 113, 143–147, 151
India Point 15
interrogations 127
Ireland 42, 53, 78, 79, 81
Italian immigration 24, 55, 59, 63, 71, 83, 119, 121–124, 128, 135, 136
Italy 25, 32, 64, 74, 79, 95, 110, 114, 117, 119, 124, 128, 133, 135, 136, 144, 145, 152

J

Jackson, Frank H. 25, 26
James W. Elwell & Company 29, 33–35
Jesus Savior Church 138
Jewish immigration 80, 81, 88, 114, 115, 131, 139
jobs 105, 123, 135, 141
Johnston 119, 145
Jones, D.H.G. 29, 34, 35, 37, 45, 54, 83, 104, 108

K

Kent, Rockwell 89
King, Clarence 104
Ku Klux Klan 86

L

LaSeyne, France 74, 100, 125
LaSpazia, Italy 114
Lazarus, Emma 153

INDEX

Lebanese immigration 85, 140
Lebanon 85, 140
Lisbon 32, 50–52, 54, 55, 57–59, 71, 72, 85, 97, 112, 113, 123, 124, 133, 136, 195
Literacy Test Act 60, 71, 80, 82, 83, 137
Long Island Sound 13, 15, 20, 34, 86, 89, 113, 152
longshoremen 145, 148
Lopes, Reverend Joseph P. 128
lumber 60, 108, 147, 148
Lusitania 53, 54
luxury ships 153

M

Madalan 109, 137
Madeira, Portugal 72, 90, 97, 104, 110, 137, 146
Madonna 19, 25, 27–31, 34, 43, 54, 68, 72, 88, 99, 103, 124, 126, 136, 145, 146, 151
Manhattan 20
Maria Sony 137
Maronites 130, 140
Marseilles, France 17–19, 25, 27–29, 32, 36, 38, 49–52, 55, 58, 70, 84, 85, 94, 97, 110, 113, 119, 121, 124, 133, 136, 139, 145, 195
Marshall, John T. 130
Martha's Vineyard 41, 103, 147
Massachusetts 15, 122, 123, 137, 144
Medeiros, Cardinal Humberto 133, 139
Mediterranean Sea 17–19, 54–57, 59, 60, 68, 70, 72, 75, 77, 82, 84, 85, 87, 93, 94, 100, 102, 104, 113–115, 119, 124, 125, 133, 140, 147, 152
Melkites 130, 140
Mellen, Charles S. 22, 24
Mercier, Cardinal Desideratus 64
Messageries Maritimes Company 112–114
Metcalf, Senator Jesse H. 95
Mexican Petroleum Corporation 148
Middle East 77, 90, 99, 113, 114, 121, 141, 146
Moshassuck River 15, 27, 58, 70
Mount Hope Bay 152
municipal pier 15, 16, 56, 60, 106, 107, 133, 147

N

Naples, Italy 28, 52, 54, 55, 70, 85, 119, 120, 123, 124, 136, 144, 189
Narragansett Bay 13–15, 28, 29, 34, 52, 68, 72, 74, 87, 103, 133, 134, 150, 152
National Archives 118, 123
national churches 67, 68, 119, 130, 138, 140, 141
National Origins Act of 1924 75, 77, 80, 82, 88, 93, 119, 121, 124
National Register of Historic Places 149, 196
Nelson, Norton W. 44, 133
Newark 34, 42
New Bedford, Rhode Island 24, 72, 108, 110, 113, 119, 122, 126, 130, 137
New England 13, 21, 24, 45, 70, 91, 95, 100, 105, 119, 137, 151, 153

217

INDEX

New Haven Railroad 13, 20–24, 27, 31, 34–38, 40, 55, 56, 69, 86, 89, 104, 105, 113, 132, 133, 136, 144, 151, 198
new immigration 20, 71, 79, 88
New Jersey 122, 123
Newport, Rhode Island 15, 87, 138, 140
1910 census 81, 82
North Africa 54, 59, 77, 99
North End (Providence) 24, 119
North Point (Bristol) 34, 41
North Providence 119
Norton, James T. 130

O

Ohio 122
Ohio Ledge 34, 41
oil 27, 60, 90, 104, 106, 144–148
"Old Immigration" 78, 79, 97
100 percent Americanism 63, 64, 65, 77
O'Neil, James 90, 134
Orthodox 67, 130, 140, 141
O'Shaunessy, Congressman George F. 42
Our Lady of the Rosary parish 128, 138
out-migration 52, 71, 91, 93

P

Page, Frank A. 45, 84
Palermo, Italy 44, 97, 119, 124, 136, 195
Palestine 80, 114, 115, 131, 140
Passenger Act of 1882 78

Patria 17, 19, 48, 49, 57, 58, 68, 85, 87, 90, 94, 95, 106, 112–115, 119, 124, 125
"patriot acts" 64
Pawtucket, Rhode Island 15, 16, 60, 119, 128, 138, 140, 141
Pennsylvania 122, 123
"pilot war" 103, 104
Piraeus, Greece 97, 134, 195
Poland 79–81, 139
Polish immigration 80, 81
port of New York 13, 17–20, 24, 25, 27, 28, 34, 43, 45, 50–52, 54, 55, 57, 58, 60, 68, 69, 70, 74, 83, 85, 85–89, 91, 100, 115, 117, 119, 121, 123–125, 134, 136, 143–145, 149–152
Portugal 51, 59, 68, 70, 74, 79, 90, 95, 110, 113, 117, 137, 138, 144, 152, 197
Portuguese immigration 24, 25, 34, 60, 63, 71, 72, 83, 90, 91, 119, 121–124, 128, 130, 136–138
Pothier, Governor Aram J. 39, 49
Priest, Samuel and Pearl 88, 89, 149
Prohibition 134
Protestant 67, 68, 86, 141
Providence Board of Trade 27, 37, 101, 108, 152
Providence Chamber of Commerce 42, 49, 55, 69–72, 83, 101, 108, 152
Providence County 86, 135
Providence Customs House 126, 144, 145
Providence Fire Department 69, 105
Providence Gas Company 88, 149

Index

Providence Journal 25, 27, 35, 36, 59, 70, 84, 87, 88, 90, 93–95, 100, 103, 104, 108, 110, 113, 126, 127, 131–134, 143, 143–146, 152
Providence Line 113, 152
Providence (magazine) 101, 108, 127
Providence River 15
Providence (ship) 47, 49, 54, 68, 72–74, 85, 98, 104, 107, 108, 112–114, 119, 124, 125
Providence-Worcester Railroad 133

Q

Quaglia, Reverend Leonardo 128
quarantine 34, 41, 42, 126, 127
Quebec, Canada 23, 39, 123

R

racing 84, 103
Rebello, Reverend Antonio 128, 138
Red Scare 65, 67, 127
Reid, Dr. James P. 67
religious persecution 60, 79, 85, 131, 135, 139–141
Rhode Island Hospital Trust Bank 132
Rhode Island Legal Aid Society 68, 132
Rochambeau 110, 112, 113
Roma 19, 34, 41, 42, 47, 52, 54, 55, 57–61, 68, 85, 91, 94, 95, 99, 100, 120, 124, 125, 147
Romania 85, 89, 97, 132
Romanian immigration 85, 130, 131, 139, 140
Russia 63, 67, 79, 80, 81, 131, 139

S

Sabin Point 32
Sant'Anna 33, 34, 49, 50, 53, 54, 59
Scalabrinian Fathers 128
Seaconnet Coal Company 148
Seaman's Act 55
Seekonk River 15, 70
Serpa, Reverend Antonio 128
Sevenitas 146
Shepard Company 150
Sicily 97, 124, 195
Silver Lake (Providence) 24, 119, 128
Silverman, Archibald 130, 131
Sisters of St. Dorothy 128
Southern New England Railroad 13, 21, 23, 55, 104, 151
South Providence 29, 31, 131, 140
Spain 17, 32, 144
Spanish immigration 139
Sprague Energy 148
St. Anthony's Church (Pawtucket) 128, 138
St. Anthony's Church (West Warwick) 138
State Harbor Improvement Commission 37, 49, 53, 69
State Pier Number 1 15, 31, 36–43, 53, 60, 68–71, 84, 88, 90, 91, 100, 105–108, 126–128, 131, 132, 140, 144, 145, 148, 153
St. Bartholomew's Church 128
St. Basil's Melkite Church 140
steerage passengers 18, 19, 28, 29, 37, 43, 110, 125, 128, 133, 137
St. Elias's Melkite Church 140
St. Elizabeth's Church 138

INDEX

St. Ephraim's Orthodox Church 141
St. Francis Xavier's Church 128, 138
St. George's Maronite Catholic Church 140
St. John's Ukrainian Orthodox Church 140
St. John the Baptist Romanian Orthodox Church 140
St. Mary's Syrian Orthodox Church 141
St. Michael's (Azores) 51, 54, 134, 139
storms 72, 74, 87, 93, 94
stowaways 133, 134
St. Raphael Society 128
St. Rocco's Church 145
St. Sahag and St. Mesrob Church 141
St. Spyridon's Greek Orthodox Church 140
St. Vartanantz Armenian Church 141
St. Vincent (Cape Verde) 104
St. Vincent de Paul Society 130
Sweeney, James 132
Syracuse (Sicily), Italy 97
Syria 85, 140, 144

T

Terminal Warehouse Company 150
Tillinghast, Anna C.M. 95
Titanic 23, 94
tourism 99, 100
Travelers Aid 89, 131
troop ship 33, 59, 69, 115
Turkey 100, 124, 144
typhus fever 41

U

U-boat 47, 49, 53, 55–57, 59, 60, 75, 83
Ukraine 85, 140
Ukrainian immigration 80, 85, 130, 140
Union of Christian Work 67
United States Army Corps of Engineers 71
unrestricted submarine warefare 59, 60
U.S. Congress 25, 42, 53, 55, 75, 78, 80, 83, 88, 151

V

Venezia 19, 34, 38, 40, 53, 58, 68, 145
Ventrone, Frank and A.E. 145, 146
Vernet, M. Paul 72
Vernon, Eugene G. 99
Vervena, Consul Mariano 25, 49, 64, 71, 84, 128, 132, 144, 145
Vidal, Laurent 74, 88
Votolato, John 145

W

Warren, Rhode Island 119
West Africa 17, 28, 109
Westerly, Rhode Island 119
West Warwick, Rhode Island 119, 138
whale fishery 122, 137
Wilkes Barre Pier 147
Wilson, President Woodrow 60, 63, 132
Woonasquatucket River 15, 58, 70

Woonsocket, Rhode Island 39, 119, 123, 140
World War I 20, 33, 45, 47, 49, 50, 52, 55, 58–65, 68, 69, 71, 72, 74, 75, 78, 79, 100, 101, 114, 117, 120, 124, 125, 140, 143, 146, 151

Y

Yates, Elizabeth Upham 132

ABOUT THE AUTHORS

WILLIAM J. JENNINGS JR.

Dr. William J. Jennings Jr. was born in Pawtucket, Rhode Island, on March 30, 1943, and has lived all his life in his native state. He was educated in Pawtucket public schools and at Providence College, where he received his bachelor's (1965), master's (1966) and doctorate (1986) degrees. His doctoral dissertation was directed by Dr. Patrick T. Conley and is entitled "The Prince of Pawtucket: A Study of the Politics of Thomas P. McCoy." Dr. Jennings was also a graduate of the Munson Institute at Mystic Seaport, which focuses on our nation's maritime history. Dr. Jennings taught history at Central Falls High School, where he served as social studies department chair, and at Immaculate Conception Catholic Regional School and Saint Raphael Academy before retiring in July 2010. He has maintained a lifelong interest in the history of his native state and America's maritime past. Currently, Dr. Jennings volunteers at Mystic Seaport, where he interprets America's relationship to the sea.

PATRICK T. CONLEY

Patrick T. Conley holds a Bachelor of Arts from Providence College, a Master of Arts and doctorate from the University of Notre Dame with highest honors and a juris doctorate from Suffolk University Law School.

About the Authors

He has published twenty-six books, as well as dozens of scholarly articles on history, law, ethnic studies, religion, real estate development, politics and political science.

The youngest person ever to attain the rank of full professor at Providence College, Dr. Conley also practices law and manages a real estate development business. He has served as chairman of the Rhode Island Bicentennial Commission, chairman and founder of the Providence Heritage Commission, chairman and founder of the Rhode Island Publications Society and general editor of the Rhode Island Ethnic Heritage Pamphlet Series. In 1977, he founded the Rhode Island Heritage Commission. Dr. Conley was also chairman of the Rhode Island Bicentennial of the Constitution Foundation and chairman of the U.S. Constitutional Council. He is also a past president of the Rhode Island Senior Olympics project.

In May 1995, Conley was inducted into the Rhode Island Heritage Hall of Fame—one of a handful of living Rhode Islanders who have been accorded that honor—and he has served as Hall of Fame president since 2003.

In the past year, Conley was named Rhode Island's first historian laureate and designated an All-American in the masters' javelin throw by the USA Track and Field Association.

The father of six children and the grandfather of seven, Conley lives in Bristol, Rhode Island, with his wife, Gail, and their Maltese, Bridget.